THE GALVESTON-HOUSTON PACKET
STEAMBOATS ON BUFFALO BAYOU

Andrew W. Hall

THE
History
PRESS

Published by The History Press
Charleston, SC 29403
www.historypress.net

Copyright © 2012 by Andrew W. Hall
All rights reserved

Front cover, top: Sternwheel packet *St. Clair* at the Houston landing, circa 1867. *Houston Metropolitan Research Center, Houston Public Library /San Jacinto Museum of History.* *Front cover, bottom:* Detail of William Aiken Walker's 1874 depiction of Galveston harbor, showing (left background) a Buffalo Bayou packet, possibly *Diana,* and (center) a cotton barge being towed by a steam tug. *Galveston and Texas History Center, Rosenberg Library, Galveston.*

Back cover: Houston Direct Navigation Co. boat *Lizzie* loading cotton at Houston, circa 1872. *Houston Metropolitan Research Center, Houston Public Library.*

First published 2012

Manufactured in the United States

ISBN 978.1.60949.591.6

Library of Congress CIP data applied for.

Notice: The information in this book is true and complete to the best of our knowledge. It is offered without guarantee on the part of the author or The History Press. The author and The History Press disclaim all liability in connection with the use of this book.

All rights reserved. No part of this book may be reproduced or transmitted in any form whatsoever without prior written permission from the publisher except in the case of brief quotations embodied in critical articles and reviews.

For Becki, Faith and Emily Faith

CONTENTS

Acknowledgements	7
1. Arroyo Cibolo	11
2. Snags	27
3. Gone to Texas	39
4. Years of Growth and Stability	49
5. The Texas Marine Department	63
6. Rebuilding	83
7. Morgan Moves In	93
8. The Final Years	103
Appendix: Steamboats Running on Buffalo Bayou	115
Notes	123
Bibliography	133
Index	139
About the Author	144

ACKNOWLEDGEMENTS

This volume had its genesis more than twenty years ago when I was on the staff of the Texas Maritime Museum in Rockport. My friend and colleague Jerry W. Moore and I developed an exhibit on Texas steamboats. The exhibit idea got a little out of hand before it was all done—it included a full-scale mockup of a steamboat pilothouse, complete with an eight-foot-diameter wheel and working bell signals—but it was hell's own fun pulling it all together. Though I'd grown up on the Texas coast, in a town that owed much of its early development to inland steam navigation, it was a story that had not often been told. I was hooked.

Two public archives have proved to be invaluable in doing the research reflected in this volume. The Houston Metropolitan Research Center at the Houston Public Library provided many of the materials upon which the initial research was based, including vertical file clippings and images, several of which appear in this work. Archivist Doug Weiskopf, in particular, provided considerable and eager assistance, tracking down half-remembered image collections and obscure references. Doug's own specialty is historic railroads, so it's hard to know if his enthusiasm about Buffalo Bayou steamboats was real or feigned, but either way, it helped propel some of my initial research, and so is to be greatly appreciated.

The other crucial archival source, naturally, is the Galveston and Texas History Center at Rosenberg Library in Galveston. The folks there have been consistently helpful and supportive of this project and willing to make extra effort in locating sources. In addition to Head of Special Collections

Acknowledgements

Casey Greene, other Rosenberg staffers who have assisted with this project include Carol Wood, Mary Magdalena Hernandez, Jenna deGraffenried, Julia Dunn, Shelly Kelly and Anna Peebler. The Galveston and Texas History Center stands as one of the preeminent historical archives in the state, and it has been my great fortune to have such a resource to guide me in this and other areas of research.

In addition to archival research, much of my understanding and appreciation of inland steam navigation has come from close examination and investigation of actual steamboat wrecks from the period. Almost all of the boats discussed in this volume are considered to be of the "Western Rivers" type, a distinctly American class of steam vessel whose design and operation was uniquely suited to the conditions of the rivers in the "West," as it was understood in the early nineteenth century, encompassing the Ohio, Mississippi and Missouri Rivers and their tributaries.

Through affiliation with the Texas Historical Commission, the Institute of Nautical Archaeology, the PAST Foundation and the Southwest Underwater Archaeology Society, I've had the opportunity to visit, record and help interpret steamboat wrecks dating as far back as the 1830s, spanning Texas from the Rio Grande to the Sabine to the Red River. Two of these boats—*A.S. Ruthven* and *Mary Conley*—themselves ran on Buffalo Bayou during their active careers. I was fortunate, as well, to be part of the team from the PAST Foundation that was first to examine the Red River wreck later identified as *Heroine*, one of the earliest examples of a Western Rivers steamboat. This practical, hands-on experience has given me a greater appreciation for the way the boats were built, how they operated and the hazards they faced.

In this fieldwork, I've benefited tremendously from three persons, in particular, who each in succession held the position of state marine archaeologist with the Texas Historical Commission: Barto Arnold, Steve Hoyt and Amy Borgens. Each of these three has offered resources, answered questions and generally helped shape my understanding of the subject. With as much as they have helped my own work, I hope that I've been able to contribute to their work at least a little bit.

Many other individuals have provided assistance and encouragement along the way. These include the late Pam Puryear of Navasota, the late Captain Alan L. Bates of Louisville, Captain Lexi Palmore, Layne Hedrick, Tom Oertling, Randy Jones, Laura Landry, Jim Hauser, Annalies Corbin and Sheli O. Smith. In particular, I want to thank my friend Edward T. Cotham Jr., author of *Battle on the Bay: The Civil War Struggle for Galveston* and other works, for his persistent encouragement and well-considered guidance.

Acknowledgements

Ed was good enough to read parts of the manuscript and make critical corrections, for which I am truly grateful. My fellow Civil War blogger and author James M. Schmidt has been a valuable sounding board for this work, based both on his experience as an author and his knowledge of Galveston in the mid-nineteenth century. Jim also helped review parts of the manuscript, which I appreciate greatly.

Finally, this work would not exist without the patience and guidance of my editors at The History Press, Becky LeJeune and Darcy Mahan. They and the rest of the staff at The History Press provided encouragement, guidance and the benefit of their experience through this process. They make me look good.

Supplemental materials, including technical background on the steamboats that ran on Buffalo Bayou, may be found at the author's website: **www.maritimetexas.net**.

Chapter 1

ARROYO CIBOLO

There was no romance in these stories.
—Historian Keith Guthrie, describing the hazards of navigation on Galveston Bay

The influx of Anglo-American settlers into Texas, which began in the 1820s and continued through the late nineteenth century, brought about fundamental change in the settlement and migration patterns of the region. Central to this new arrangement were the rivers that crossed the eastern half of the territory, particularly the Brazos and Colorado Rivers and Buffalo Bayou. These waterways both shaped and were shaped by the new Texians, as the people began to call themselves, changing both the cultural and physical geography of the region.

The Spanish rulers of Texas, and the Mexican governments that succeeded them from 1821, did not view rivers in the same way that the Americans would later. The Spanish settlements and outposts, largely confined to the southern and western parts of the region, did not rely significantly on waterways for the transport of people, and failed to establish a port of any significance along what is now the Texas coast.[1] Communications between the Spanish settlements depended entirely upon a series of trails, the most famous of which was the Royal Road, *el Camino Real*, which extended from Monclova and Saltillo, in present-day Mexico, through San Antonio to Nacogdoches. In large part, this landlocked approach was due to the rigidity of the Spanish colonial administration, which prohibited trade with outsiders and restricted ports of entry to two—Vera Cruz for seaborne traffic and Nacogdoches for overland travelers.[2]

During its short rule over Texas (1821–36), the Mexican government made a critical change in policy that ultimately would cause it to lose control over the province altogether: the Mexicans actively worked to establish colonization in Texas, notably by allowing Stephen F. Austin to found a colony at San Felipe on the Brazos River. Austin's settlers, and those that came after them, would very quickly establish river navigation as the primary and essential means of transportation in what would become Anglo-American Texas.

Roads in Texas in the early nineteenth century were almost uniformly abysmal. Often they were little more than expanded animal paths cut through the brush, poorly built and indifferently maintained. Although they were usually passable in the dry season, during the wet months in the winter and spring they quickly deteriorated into muddy morasses in which freight wagons and carriages would sink to their axles. Newly formed stagecoach lines sometimes quoted different fares for dry weather and wet, and one passenger in the days of the Texas Republic later recalled that "the passenger who travelled in these [coaches] had to work his way by carrying a fence rail on his shoulder…to pry the vehicle out of mudholes in order to reach his destination at all."[3] Frederick Law Olmstead, following the immigrant wagon trains through eastern Texas, observed that his route "could hardly be called a road. It was only a way where people had passed along before. Each man had taken such a path as suited him, turning aside to avoid, on high ground, the sand, and on low ground, the mud."[4]

River navigation offered a promising alternative to overland travel, but even it presented substantial challenges. Texas rivers were small and shallow, often clogged with snags and brush. They often overflowed their banks during the spring rains or ran almost dry during the summer and fall. At their mouths, they usually developed sandbars that impeded navigation and kept out all but the smallest vessels.[5] Nevertheless, these were challenges that could be overcome, and the new Texians devoted tremendous energy and ingenuity to make Texas' rivers viable routes for the transport of people, agricultural commodities and manufactured goods.

Buffalo Bayou rises in Fort Bend County, west of present-day Houston, and runs almost due east until it meets the San Jacinto River near the head of Galveston Bay. The name of the stream is at least as old as European settlement along its banks; the name first appears in an 1828 deed, written in Spanish, in which one of Stephen F. Austin's colonists transfers a parcel of land to Austin himself. The property is described as being "*sur del Arroyo Cibalo [Cibolo] con[o]cido on Ingles por el nombre de* Buffalo Bayou"—"south of Cibolo Creek, known in English by the name Buffalo Bayou."[6]

Bison bison, as the American buffalo is scientifically known, was not the only inhabitant of the banks of the stream. The land along the Texas coastal plain tends to be flat and divided in roughly equal parts of deciduous woodland and open prairie. In addition to buffalo, a visitor in the early days, passing through in the spring, described a "wet and somewhat boggy prairie," scattered with herds of wild horses and deer.[7] Smaller, much less welcome creatures were to be found in abundance, as well; that same traveler noted that readers should never take a bed on one of the ranches that were beginning to dot the prairie, for

> *they are general and particular repositories of vermin and insects, and if you enter them, you will most likely encounter whole tribes of "ugly customers," which, like the plagues of Egypt, come into the very bed chambers, while perchance you will be discomforted by some dirty traveler, who makes his way after you, and whose corporation, it may be, has not felt the "sweet influences" of a lavation since the Mosaic flood, and who, sans cérémonie, becomes your bedfellow, and mayhap inflict upon you one of the aforesaid abominations of Egypt in the form of some filthy and disgusting disease. Rather take to your buffalo robe and blanket, and "upon the outer wall" repose in peace.*[8]

Plant life was lush and vibrant. Nicholas Clopper, one of the earliest American immigrants to then-Mexican Texas, wrote that the bayou was the most remarkable that he had seen. It had the look of a dug canal, with the timber shrubbery reaching right to the water's edge,

> *which overhang its grassy banks & dip & reflect their variegated hues in its unruffled waters. These impending shrubs are in places overtopped by the evergreen magnolia…The banks of this stream are secured from the lavings of the water by what are here termed "cypress knees"…apparently exuberances of cypress roots* [that] *shoot up along the margin of the waters to the height of 3 & 4 feet…So closely & regularly are they often found standing in lines as to resemble piles driven in purposely as security against the innovation of the tide.*[9]

Frederick Benjamin Page, the traveler who had warned against vermin when bedding down at isolated ranches on the plain, noted that the bayou's banks were "covered with fruit trees and shrubbery of enormous growth." He recorded magnolias, evergreen pines, cypress, the trumpet vine catalpa, wild grape, honeysuckle and passionflower.[10]

The old-timers also agreed that, in the early days, Buffalo Bayou was deep, clearer and more full of aquatic life than it later became. Dr. S.O. Young, who was born in Houston in 1848, recalled many years later that in his youth, there was a little German settlement called Hillendahl on the bayou, a few miles upstream from Houston, where one of the main events each summer was a big fish fry. Two weeks before the day of the event, the settlement's boys would stake out a likely stretch of the bayou and dive in to clear snags and other obstructions that would foul their seine net. This was done well in advance, to let the spooked fish return to their accustomed haunts. Then on the chosen Sunday morning, the citizens of Hillendahl would converge on a clear spot on the bank of the bayou. While the women set up cooking fires, the young men retired to the woods and changed into old clothes. Emerging again, the men took up the seine and, aligning themselves from one bank to the other, used the net to sweep up hundreds of fish.

One day, though, the net got caught in a deep hole. They pulled the seine first one way, then another, to no avail. Eventually one young man dived into the hole and struggled to get the net loose from what seemed an enormous log. Then the "log" moved, and he realized the seine had been caught up on a huge alligator. Young recalled that the young man "came up like a rocket, rose way out of the water and made for the shore, shouting at the top of his voice the German equivalent for alligator." After much argument and discussion about what to do, it was finally decided to use brute force to haul out the crocodilian. Everyone on the shore took hold of the net and tugged with all their might. With much effort they dragged the creature out of the hole and onto the bank. To this point the alligator had not torn the net, but now he took to thrashing about with his tail at one end and his jaws at the other. The men descended on the poor beast with axes and shovels and any other heavy instruments close to hand, destroying whatever was left of the net in the process. After it was all over, Young recalled, "they realized what foolish capers they had cut and laughed heartily at each others' antics. It was the best and most surprising seining party I ever attended."[11]

These amphibious predators were objects of curiosity to many visitors traversing the bayou. Like the bison of the Great Plains along the route of

Steamboats on Buffalo Bayou

Buffalo Bayou in its natural state. From King's *The Southern States of North America*.

the transcontinental railroad, alligators on Buffalo Bayou were sometimes evocative symbols of a new, barely tamed wilderness. Like the bison, they too were sometimes the target of overzealous steamboat passengers, eager to test their marksmanship on the big animals.

Buffalo Bayou is fed by several smaller tributaries, the largest of which is White Oak Bayou that flows into the larger stream from the northern parts of Harris County. The confluence of these two waterways, roughly forty-seven miles downstream from Buffalo Bayou's origin, marks the site that would later be staked out as Houston and would also serve as the effective head of navigation on Buffalo Bayou. The rise and fall of the tide was barely perceptible here, but became more noticeable as one moved downstream. The bayou gradually became wider and reliably deep, ten feet or more in some places. The current on Buffalo Bayou was generally slow, but heavy rains could swell the stream and generate a rapid current. Such a flow presented an obstacle for the small, under-powered steamboats struggling to go upstream, as well as a hazard for down-bound boats that found it difficult to steer while being swept along. The naturalist John James Audubon visited Texas and, in the spring of 1837, made the trip up the bayou in the 120-ton sidewheel steamboat *Crusader*. After two days' slow progress up from Galveston, the boat stopped for the night along the banks of the bayou near the house of a settler named Batterson. It had rained all that day and was still raining the next morning. Anxious to be on their way, Audubon; his twenty-five-year-old son, John; and their friend Edward Harris set out on their own in the steamboat's gig. Rains had swollen the bayou, causing it to rise as much as six feet. "The neighboring prairies were partly covered with water," Audubon wrote, "[and] there was a wild and desolate look cast upon the surrounding scenery." The three men eventually reached the town site of Houston, wet and exhausted; it had taken them eight full hours to row twelve miles against the current.[12]

Below the site of Houston the stream continued, wending back and forth in alternately sharp and wide turns, but generally almost due east. The abbé Emmanuel Domenech, a French clergyman traveling through Texas and Mexico, took the route up Buffalo Bayou in the early years after the steamboat trade had been established. He set out one sweltering day in late July from Galveston, heading up the bay toward the bayou and Houston, beyond:

> *The sky was a very furnace of fire, and the bay sparkled like a polished mirror. In the distance, a few bushes scattered on islets displayed their grey*

Steamboats on Buffalo Bayou

John James Audubon. *Library of Congress.*

outline on an horizon raised to a white-heat temperature. Arrived at the extremity of the bay, we entered the little Buffalo river, bordered with reeds and bulrushes, in the midst of which herons, and cranes, and thousands of ducks were disputing. By-and-by the banks increasing in height, approached so near each other, and formed so many narrow and tortuous windings, that at every instant the boat was caught either by the bow or the stern. At length the high lands appeared, covered with magnolias with their large white flowers and delicious perfumes. Grey and red squirrels leaped from branch to branch, while mocking-birds and cardinals imparted life and language to these wonderful solitudes.[13]

If the abbé was impressed with the pastoral beauty of the scene, some of his fellow passengers took a more pragmatic view. When Domenech, caught in the moment, exclaimed, "What magnificent trees!" a Kentuckian standing nearby replied, "Yes, they would make fine wood for building purposes."[14]

In fact, neither the abbé nor the Kentuckian may have appreciated one of the dangers represented by the trees, that of "snagging." As the banks of any river or stream gradually erode, trees along the edge occasionally fall into the stream. Some of these will eventually make their way to the sea, but many will strike a submerged obstacle and become embedded in the bottom of the stream. Because trees tended to drift with their broad, leafy canopies oriented downstream, very often the solid, heavy trunk of the tree ended up

1850s caricature of a steamboat being snagged. *Harper's Magazine.*

pointed upstream, into the current. Sometimes the bare end of the trunk would be visible above the surface, rising and falling with the motion of the water; these snags were known as "sawyers," as they mimicked the up-and-down motion of men working in a saw pit. More often, though, the snag would lie just below the surface, waiting patiently for a boat to impale itself on it. Striking a snag usually resulted in broken and knocked-in hull planks and flooding, at a minimum; the extremely lightweight construction of the steamboat's hull offered no real protection against such a strike.

In the early years of steamboating on the Ohio and Mississippi, snags accounted for at least half of all steamboat losses; taken with other obstructions, they accounted for nearly three-fifths of all steamboat accidents to mid-century.[15] Fortunately, snaggings rarely resulted in large-scale loss of life. They generally happened in shallow water, allowing passengers, crew and soggy cargo to be evacuated in an orderly fashion. Very often, as well, a snagged boat could be refloated, repaired and put back into service relatively quickly. Buffalo Bayou would ultimately claim only a handful of boats permanently lost to snagging, but the snags would remain a serious hazard throughout the nineteenth century.

Twenty-five or thirty miles below the town site that would become Houston, following the winding course of the stream, Buffalo Bayou makes a sharp swing to the south, around the flat, marshy plain of San Jacinto, where the Texian army met and defeated the Mexican army under Santa Anna in 1836, winning Texas' independence from Mexico City. It is here that the San Jacinto River merges with Buffalo Bayou, effectively marking the terminus of both waterways. The merged waters flow through a broad estuary, perhaps ten miles long—or fifteen miles, following the curves and bends of the natural channel—and varying in width from one to two miles or more. This estuary, known as San Jacinto Bay, is dotted with small islands and sandbars. At the lower end of this estuary, marking the head of Galveston Bay proper, is a broad finger of land that originally took the name of Clopper's Point. Nicholas Clopper had been one of the first to recognize the potential for navigation on Buffalo Bayou, and in 1826, he purchased the land from Stephen F. Austin. Clopper platted out a town site, but the settlement never took off, and the land was eventually sold to James Morgan. The location is still known as Morgan's Point, but one landmark that would carry Clopper's name was a sand bar across the lower end of San Jacinto Bay. Clopper's Bar was particularly troublesome, since it tended to shift its position slightly from year to year, requiring constant care and vigilance on the part of pilots trying to negotiate its shoal water.[16] Even before effective dredging became possible, it was suggested that boats passing over the bar drop weighted buoys to mark their routes; steamboats following later could follow the same route, gradually rubbing a navigable channel through the bar.[17]

Past Clopper's Bar lies the open expanse of Galveston Bay. The bay extends some twenty-six miles to the south-southeast, where it empties into the Gulf of Mexico. The main body of Galveston Bay is roughly ten miles across, with smaller, contiguous bays branching off from it. To the northeast is Trinity Bay and the estuary of the Trinity River, which flows down from East Texas; to the east is East Bay, separating the Bolivar Peninsula from the mainland; and to the southwest is West Bay, extending down toward San Luis Pass at the far western end of Galveston Island.

Galveston Bay is naturally shallow, in most places no more than six or eight feet deep. This would present no particular challenge to steamboats, which even with a full cargo typically drew little more than five feet, but the bay was also crossed by several oyster reefs, enormous colonies of the mollusks that extended for miles. These oyster reefs were typically aligned roughly east-west, to take optimum advantage of the north-south ebb and flow of the tide, a current that brought clean water and nutrients to the bivalve animals. Over centuries, untold generations of oysters would spawn and, seeking a hard surface on which to attach on an otherwise sandy bottom, affix themselves to other oyster shells nearby. Over time, this process created a series of calcified oyster reefs—hard, almost rock-

The Galveston–Houston Packet

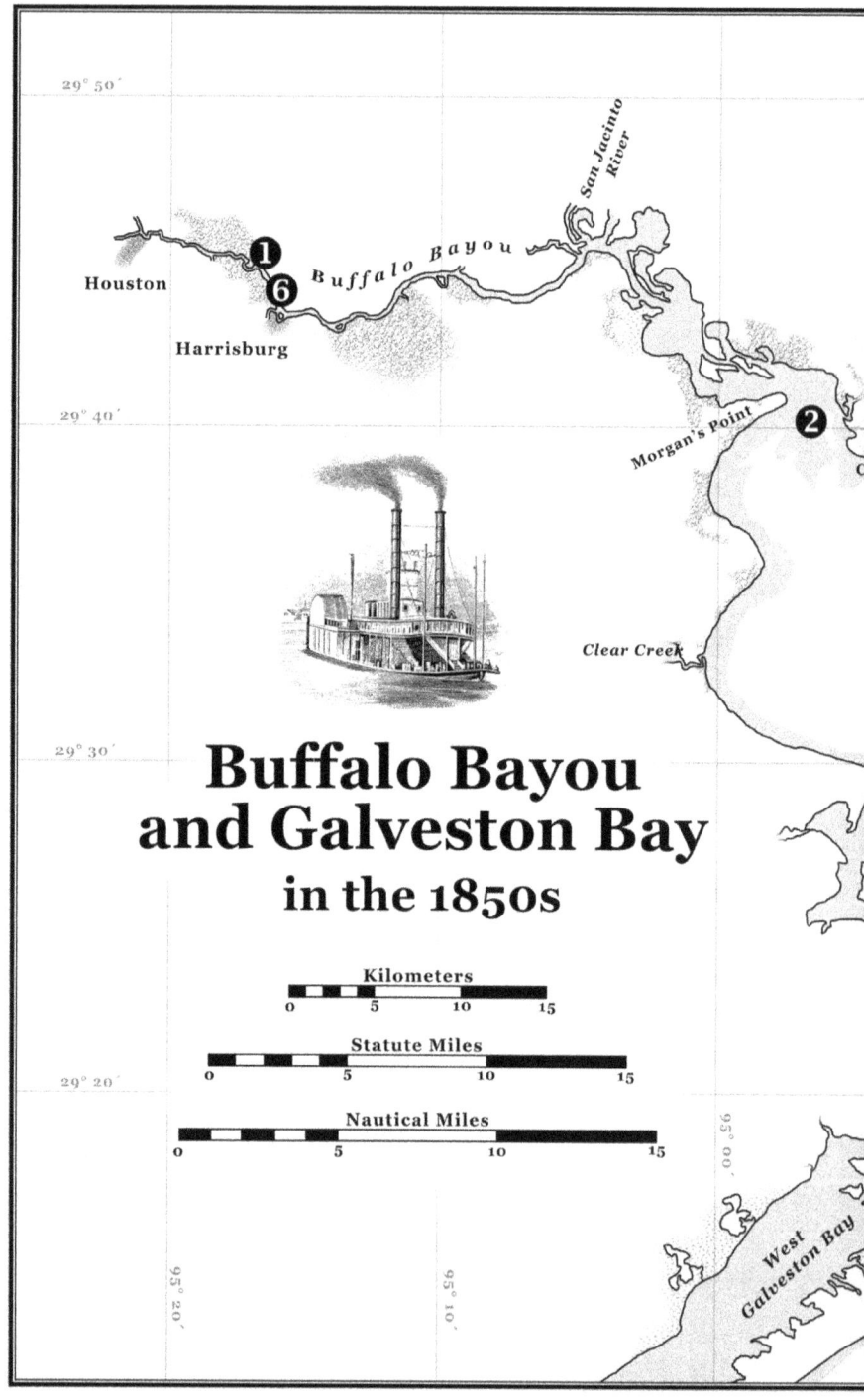

Buffalo Bayou and Galveston Bay in the 1850s

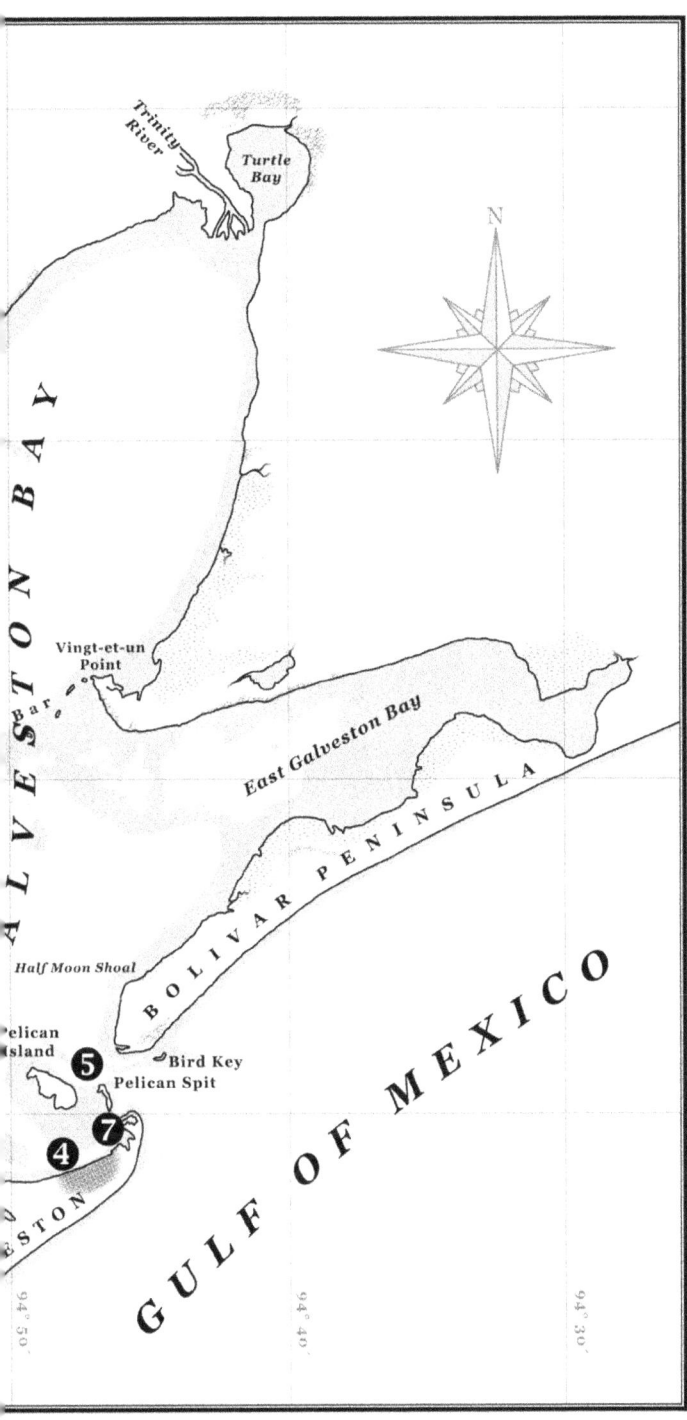

Map showing the general configuration of Buffalo Bayou, Galveston Bay, and events mentioned in the text. *Map by the author.*

like obstructions that could easily cripple a boat. The most important of these oyster reefs was Red Fish Bar, a nine-mile-long reef curving in a gentle, east-west arc stretching completely across Galveston Bay, almost exactly halfway between Clopper's Bar and Galveston Island. Red Fish Bar could, on occasion, cause significant damage to vessels, and at least one steamboat, *Ellen P. Frankland*, would be wrecked on the obstruction in the 1840s.[18] Both Clopper's Bar and Red Fish Bar could be crossed regularly by vessels drawing less than four feet, but this depth of water varied with the tide and weather. Sometime in the early 1850s, both navigational hazards were marked with small lighthouses.[19]

The large, open expanse of Galveston Bay would present its own challenges. The land all around is low and flat—so low, in fact, that to an observer on the deck of a steamboat, the shore at the far end of the bay is invisible, below the horizon. This presented a different sort of hazard to steamboatmen, whose craft were of very shallow draft, with tall, lightweight structures that easily caught the wind. Unlike within the narrow confines of Buffalo Bayou, where high banks and vegetation provided some protection against high wind and waves, when out on the bay, steamboats were extremely vulnerable to heavy weather, which could come at any time of the year. In the spring and summer, there were heavy thunderstorms, often accompanied by tornados or waterspouts. In the late summer and early autumn, there was always the threat of a tropical storm or hurricane, whose winds and storm surge would reach high up into the bay. In the winter, there was the threat of "northers," a distinctive regional weather phenomenon described by one traveler in the 1840s:

> *They most frequently occur after a few days of damp dull weather, and generally about once a fortnight. Their approach is known by a dark bank rising on the horizon, and gradually overspreading the heavens. The storm bursts forth with wonderful suddenness and tremendous violence and generally lasts forty-eight hours; the wind after that period veers round to the east and southward, and the storm gradually abates. During the continuance of a norther, the cold is intense, and the wind so penetrating, it is almost impossible to keep oneself warm.*[20]

The loss of the small, 120-ton steamboat *C.K. Hall* in October 1871 dramatically showed the dangers of being caught in the open during foul weather on the bay. The boat had come out of Cedar Bayou, at the bottom end of San Jacinto Bay, on the evening of Friday, September 29.

There were reportedly ten or twelve men on board, along with a cargo of fifty thousand bricks, all bound for Galveston. There was a strong chop on the bay, so Captain Le Clere anchored at the head of Galveston Bay, waiting for the weather to settle. Unbeknownst to Le Clere and his crew, a severe storm was bearing down on the upper Texas coast. Meteorological records are fragmentary, but it was likely a tropical storm by the modern definition. It brought with it heavy rains, howling winds and a storm surge, blown by winds from the north, that inundated much of Galveston. The storm grew in intensity through Tuesday, October 3. The wind blew full from the north, suggesting the center of the storm passed somewhere to the east of the island.

Aboard *C.K. Hall*, on October 2, as the seas and wind began to rise, the crew began jettisoning the brick cargo and successfully discarded almost all of it over the side. But the boat continued to pitch violently, and the anchor's chain cable broke. The crew put out a smaller anchor, but in the increasing wind, Captain Le Clere feared that the boat would be swamped. He ordered the cable cut, and the little steamboat began drifting before the gale. Soon the upper works of the boat began to break apart. A passenger named Burlander and an employee of the brickyard were washed off the deck, followed soon after by the boat's engineers, Richard Nagle and a Mr. Taylor. Finally, the rest of the cabin broke apart, sweeping the remaining men into the sea. Crew member Otto Lassen alone made it to shore alive, reaching land about twenty miles up the bay from Galveston, from where he walked overland to the railway line and was found. Seven corpses later washed ashore between Clear Creek and Edward's Point, including those of Captain Le Clere and Richard Nagle.[21]

The loss of *C.K. Hall* and most of her crew was not particularly unusual during that period; numerous other vessels were lost or severely damaged in that same storm. But it does point to the practical, everyday dangers of navigation on Galveston Bay in the nineteenth century. Boats like *C.K. Hall* and their crews were engaged in a difficult and often dangerous business. As the late Texas coastal historian Keith Guthrie wrote, "There was no romance in these stories."[22]

The southern terminus of the Buffalo Bayou route was the city of Galveston, located on the bay side of a thirty-mile-long barrier sand island. Like the rest of the land surrounding Galveston Bay, Galveston Island is extremely low, with a maximum natural elevation of no more than eight feet above normal high tide. Inundations of large parts of the island were commonplace in the nineteenth century, occurring particularly in the late summer and fall with the emergence of heavy weather and tropical storms. It was not uncommon for the sea to wash completely over the island when a major storm pushed a storm surge ahead of it that might reach ten feet or more.[23]

Galveston had been settled by a series of adventurers in the early years of the century, including the pirate Jean Laffite, after being forced to move his base of operations west from Louisiana. Though the Texas coast is scattered with bays and inlets, Galveston was the only one that offered a sheltered, deep-water harbor that could accommodate the larger classes of ships that plied the Gulf of Mexico. Galveston harbor, a long, narrow waterway running parallel to the shore on the bay side of the island, was up to twenty-four feet deep for most of its length. Long, wooden piers were built out from the shore on the bay side into the deeper water, with long wharves built at right angles to them (i.e., parallel to the harbor and the shore), allowing deep-draft vessels to tie up directly at the wharf to load and unload passengers and cargo. Over time, these T-headed piers were gradually connected to one another, forming a continuous set of wharf frontage. The shallow water in between the line of wharf frontage was gradually filled in, creating the Galveston waterfront that survives to the present.

The eastern end of Galveston Island curved northward, making a sort of fishhook shape pointing up into Galveston Bay. The tip of the hook commanded an unobstructed view of the entrance to the bay, and from the earliest days of settlement on the island was the site of a military battery of one sort or another. Inevitably, this geographic feature came to be known as Fort Point, a name it retains today, even though that location no longer remains the easternmost point of the island. Between Fort Point and the end of the Bolivar Peninsula, over two miles away to the northeast, lies an open expanse of water where Galveston Bay meets the Gulf of Mexico. This wide area, continually scoured by the ebb and flow of the tide between the bay and the Gulf, is deep and forms an open anchorage. This roadstead, which came to be known as Bolivar Roads, offered a somewhat less-sheltered anchorage than the harbor but provided ample room for seagoing vessels to anchor while awaiting a cargo or sitting out a precautionary quarantine imposed by port officials on ships newly arrived from areas known to be afflicted with epidemics of contagious disease, such as yellow fever. The anchorage would also serve for a time, after the Civil War, as a place where Buffalo Bayou steamboats would transfer passengers and cargo from seagoing steamships, in an effort to avoid the wharfage fees at Galveston.[24]

Beyond the anchorage of Bolivar Roads lay one last, unseen barrier between the bay and the open Gulf of Mexico. A wide, semi-circular sandbar, known simply as "the Bar," formed an underwater obstruction for vessels entering and leaving Galveston and the bay. Long Gulf swells, driven by strong, onshore sea breezes from the southeast, would sometimes strike this low, submerged ridge, deflecting their lateral energy upward into breaking waves of foam. Mariners were cautioned to watch for these breakers as a telltale sign of shallow water. It was this bar—not the depth of the harbor—that limited the size of vessels that could enter Galveston. Ships drawing twelve feet or less usually had little difficulty getting over the bar, but larger vessels were obliged to bring on board a pilot, a licensed, local mariner with particular knowledge of the underwater topography, tides and currents, to maneuver their way into the bay. A strong north wind, blowing for several days straight, would also reduce the depth of water over the bar, making its traverse even more hazardous. Matilda Charlotte Houstoun, who would pen one of the most detailed early accounts of traveling on Buffalo Bayou, found herself in just such a predicament when she and her husband first arrived at Galveston in their sailing yacht, *Dolphin*:

> *We spent at least three hours* [waiting for a pilot], *shortening the time as well as we could in abusing all the government authorities indiscriminately, and pilots in particular. At length, however, to our great relief, a large steamer, the* New York, *which we had observed some time previously occupied in getting up her steam, was seen coming towards us; her high-pressure engine was puffing and blowing, like some huge elephant out of breath, and her deck covered with curious passengers.*
>
> *When she had arrived within speaking-trumpet distance, the captain hailed us through this instrument, which is still in general use in American ships, and gave us the welcome information that he had a pilot on board. We were delighted; as we now saw some chance of coming to an anchor that day: the prospect of spending another night standing off and on was by no means agreeable.*
>
> *Before taking leave of us, the Captain, in a true Yankee spirit of "making an operation," offered to tow us over the bar. This was on his own account, and for this piece of civility, and trifling assistance, the performance of which would have occupied him half an hour, he demanded the moderate sum of one hundred dollars!—of course the offer was declined; however, as it was made civilly, hats were mutually raised in token of amity, and the* New York *puffed back to her station in the harbour.*[25]

The Galveston–Houston Packet

Mrs. Houstoun, *Dolphin* and all aboard eventually made it into the harbor safely, though with much maneuvering of the vessel and shifting of guns and ballast, to ensure that the schooner didn't touch bottom in her progress.

The navigational hazards facing those who would navigate Galveston Bay and Buffalo Bayou were many and challenging. While some readers will be familiar with the dangers of the Mississippi or the Missouri, with their snags, sandbars and violent weather, all those things and more besides were concerns to the Texas steamboat pilot. Along with those came tides, oyster reefs, and the necessity of traversing miles of open, unsheltered waters, as well as the occasional tropical storm or hurricane. This natural environment, with its unique combination of challenges and obstacles, would end up shaping the Buffalo Bayou trade more than any other factor and, in so doing, influence the course of settlement in Texas and the West.

Chapter 2

SNAGS

Disappointment and delay have met us at every turn.
—Francis Moore, publisher of *the Telegraph and Texas Register.*

The first known steamboat on Buffalo Bayou—or anywhere else in Texas, for that matter—was one owned by a Connecticut Yankee, Henry Austin (1782–1852). Henry had taken to maritime affairs early, shipping out at the age of twelve as a cabin boy on one of his father's trading vessels for a voyage to China by way of the Falkland Islands. Upon his return, Henry learned that his father had died on another voyage, leaving him with much of the responsibility for the family's finances. Henry had abandoned the seagoing life completely by his early twenties and settled into a life as a merchant in New Haven. He was not particularly successful, though, and by 1824 was casting about for a new opportunity. It was in that year he decided to take up an offer extended by his cousin Stephen F. Austin to bring his skills as a merchant to Mexico. Stephen had established a colony of American settlers on the Texas coast but, he advised, there were ample opportunities throughout Mexico. In early 1825, Henry set up several businesses in Mexico at Jalapa, Vera Cruz, Alvarado and Nacotálpam. None turned a profit, and by the fall of 1826, Henry Austin was back in New York, determining his next venture.[26]

By the summer of 1829, Henry Austin was back in Texas, this time with a new steamboat, *Ariel*, to run on the Rio Grande. The boat was a small one, only eighty-six tons, built in New York in 1825.[27] Although the English-language paper in Stephen F. Austin's colony predicted great things for Henry Austin's new boat—the *Texas Gazette* in San Felipe opined that Henry Austin might be able to take his little steamer all the way to New Mexico under the right conditions—but on the Rio Grande, 250 miles away, Henry Austin's reality was much different. He and *Ariel* missed what should have been his most profitable season when he and his crew fell ill. He found that many locals, who had never seen a steamboat before, were afraid of the huffing, smoke-belching craft. Above all, Austin found, his New Englander's direct, fast-paced approach to business simply did not mesh with the slower, more relaxed culture of the Mexican frontier. Austin blamed his failure on the Rio Grande to the character of the Mexican temperament; what the Mexicans thought of Austin's brusque, get-it-done-yesterday approach is not recorded.[28]

In August 1830, Henry Austin and *Ariel* arrived at the mouth of the Brazos River. He liked the surrounding country but thought that the potential of navigation on the Brazos would not be met until the completion of a canal connecting that river with Galveston Bay to the east. Henry Austin applied for a large land grant near the river, and in the winter, he and *Ariel* set out for New Orleans, perhaps with the intent of having the boat refitted. Upon leaving the Brazos, though, *Ariel* struck the bar and was damaged. Austin was obliged to put in at Galveston, and he eventually ran the boat up Buffalo Bayou as far as Harrisburg. The little boat was leaking badly, her chimney knocked down and generally in disrepair. Wanting to continue his journey to New Orleans, Henry Austin left the little boat at a secluded landing on the San Jacinto River, where she eventually rotted away to kindling.[29]

Henry Austin's experience with *Ariel* was not a successful one in the conventional sense. The boat probably never turned a month's profit and proved to be a constant headache for a man who had learned the mariner's trade on the China run. Austin returned to Texas and settled on his land grant near the Brazos, which he named Bolivar. Though as a planter he took an ongoing interest in commercial navigation on the river, he was out of the shipping business for good. He died in Galveston in 1852.

But Henry Austin's legacy is more important than that of a failed merchant whose approach came just a few years too early. Austin was the first to attempt steam navigation on three different waterways—the Rio Grande River, the Brazos River and Buffalo Bayou—that would each become, within a few years, substantial routes of maritime commerce in their own right. Austin's experience demonstrated three difficult realities that would be faced by those who came after him. First, Austin discovered the challenges

Grave of Captain Henry Austin (1782–1852), Galveston. *Author's photo.*

presented by the bars, shoals and other hazards at the mouths of rivers where they emptied into the Gulf of Mexico. Second, Austin learned of the high variability of Texas rivers, which would rise and fall quickly, depending on seasonal rainfall and the topography of the region. This is particularly true the farther west and south one goes, as the climate becomes more arid and the streams more marginal for navigation; under the circumstances, Austin's choice of the Rio Grande for his initial venture with *Ariel* is ironic. Finally, Austin's experience demonstrated the fundamental lesson that would apply to early steamboating in Texas generally, and on Buffalo Bayou in particular, that success depended on perseverance, patience and luck—and even then was never a sure thing.[30]

The defeat of the Mexican army at San Jacinto in April 1836, and its subsequent retreat beyond the Rio Grande, opened the floodgates of settlement in Texas. Good, arable land was plentiful but sparsely populated. Awaiting the flood of immigrants to the newly established nation were land speculators, among them Augustus Chapman Allen (1806–1864) and his brother, John Kirby Allen (1810–1838). The Allen brothers, natives of western New York State, had settled in the far eastern part of Texas a few years before the Texas Revolution, establishing themselves (like many in that time and place) in a variety of business ventures, notably in the sale and exchange of land certificates. When the revolution came, the Allens did not join the Texian army themselves but did outfit a privateer for the defense of the Texas coast. They subsequently sold this schooner, *Brutus*, to the provisional government of Texas at their cost, where the vessel became one of the first ships in the new republic's navy.[31]

   The Allens, along with others, began investing in large tracts of land as quickly as they could. Augustus Allen had long been interested in establishing a city on Galveston Island, which sheltered the best harbor on the coast and where, as a result, attempts at settlement had occurred off and on for almost two decades. He invested in the newly formed Galveston City Company but was more interested in a project of his own. He and John looked at a variety of sites around Galveston Bay, but the most promising of those locations were already settled and either not for sale or tied up in litigation. Eventually they began looking further upstream of Harrisburg on Buffalo Bayou. They ultimately decided on a spot at the confluence of Buffalo and White Oak Bayous, a half-league (approx. 2,214 acres) land grant made to John Austin, a close friend of Stephen F. Austin. John Austin had died in 1833, and his heirs sold the property to the Allens in August 1836.[32]

With the property now secure, the Allens shrewdly chose to name their new city Houston, after the hero of San Jacinto. They immediately began advertising for the sale of lots:

> *Situated at the head of navigation…the town of Houston is located at a point on the river which must ever command the trade of the largest and richest portion of Texas. By reference to the map, it will be seen that the trade of San Jacinto, Spring Creek, New Kentucky and the Brazos, above and below Fort Bend, must necessarily come to this place, and will at this time warrant the employment of at least ONE MILLION DOLLARS of capital, and when the rich lands of this country shall be settled, a great trade will flow into it, making it, beyond all doubt, the great commercial emporium of Texas…*
>
> *Tide water runs to this place and the lowest depth of water is about six feet. Vessels from New Orleans or New York can sail without obstacle to this place, and steamboats of the largest class can run down to Galveston Island in 8 or 10 hours, in all seasons of the year. It is but a few hours sail down the bay, where one may take an excursion of pleasure and enjoy the luxuries of fish, fowl, oysters and sea bathing. Galveston harbor being the only one in which vessels drawing a large draft of water can navigate, must necessarily render the Island the great naval and commercial depot of the country.*[33]

The advertisement goes on to stress the general healthfulness of the climate, the ready availability of timber and stone for construction and the inevitability of Houston becoming the republic's primary military arsenal, its seat of government (which actually happened soon after) and its ultimate connection to other settled parts of the republic by yet-to-be-chartered railroads. It's also a remarkably brazen document, even by the truth-telling standards of land speculators, because in fact no steamboat—much less one "of the largest class"—had ever got within a half dozen miles of the place. Nonetheless, the advertisement ran for months in existing Texas papers like the Columbia *Telegraph and Texas Register*, with requests for reprint in American papers, including the New Orleans *Commercial Bulletin*, the Mobile *Advertiser*, the Washington *Globe*, the Louisville *Public Advertiser* and the New York papers the *Enquirer* and *Herald*.[34]

The Allens had claimed Houston was "situated at the head of navigation." Such a pretense couldn't be maintained forever, and by the end of 1836, the

The Galveston–Houston Packet

A highly imaginative view of Houston from a European publication of the 1840s. *Library of Congress.*

Allens began looking for a steamboat that would make good on their claim. *Laura* was a small boat, nearly new, having been completed in Louisville, Kentucky, in 1835. She was just sixty-five registered tons, eighty-five feet long and sixteen feet wide, not including the paddlewheels. Her depth of hold—the vertical distance between the underside of the deck planking and the planking over her frames at the bottom of the hull—was just barely over five feet. Her registration at New Orleans, filed in June 1835, describes *Laura* as having no masts, a single deck, a plain bow and a narrow stern that extended well out past the sternpost and rudder.[35]

Francis Richard Lubbock (1815–1905) was one of *Laura*'s passengers. Lubbock would go on to be, in turn, Texas' lieutenant governor, its governor under the Confederacy, a Confederate military officer, an aide to Confederate president Jefferson Davis, a local tax collector and Texas state treasurer. Before all that, though, he was a twenty-one-year-old South Carolinian with aspirations of making his mercantile fortune on the Texas frontier. Lubbock had initially set up his store on the Brazos River, the center of Austin's colony and American immigration into Texas, but the Allens convinced Lubbock to move his enterprise to their new town.

The party set out from Galveston in mid-January 1837. The passage up Galveston Bay was uneventful, though *Laura* was grounded on a sandbar for several days before she floated free, and they were able to resume the trip. They reached Harrisburg without further incident, but beyond that it would be difficult going. For Lubbock, the passage of the steamboat up the narrow, snag-filled stream was a young man's adventure of working hard during the day and playing hard at night:

> *No boat had ever been above this place* [Harrisburg], *and we were three days making the distance to Houston, only six miles by the dirt road, but twelve by the bayou. The slow time was in consequence of the obstructions we were compelled to remove as we progressed. We had to rig what were called Spanish windlasses on the shore to heave the logs and snags out of our way, the passengers all working faithfully. All hands on board would get out on the shore, and cutting down a tree would make of it a windlass by boring holes in it and placing it upon a support and throwing a bight of rope around it, secure one end to a tree in the rear and the other to the snags or fallen trees in the water. Then by means of the capstan bars we would turn the improvised capstan on land, and draw from the track of our steamer the obstructions. Capitalist, dignified judge, military hero,* [and] *young merchant in fine clothes from the dressiest city in the United States, all lent a helping hand. It being necessary to lie by at night, in the evenings we had a good time dancing and frolicking with the settlers on the shore, who were delighted to see "newcomers from the States."*[36]

Lubbock and several of his buddies, though, soon grew bored of life on *Laura* and, taking the steamboat's yawl, headed upstream on their own to find the new city. They actually rowed past it, up into what he later learned was White Oak Bayou. They retraced their route and soon found a muddy path cut through the brush, marked out with surveyors' stakes. "Wharves," Lubbock dryly recalled decades later, "were not in Texas." The *Telegraph and Texas Register*, which had been running the Allens' promotional ads for months, announced the arrival of *Laura* at Houston with a one-sentence notice under the intentionally understated headline "The Fact Proved."[37]

In fact, there was not much to Houston at all at that point. Lubbock found that the city consisted mostly of a smattering of tents, the largest of which, of course, served as a saloon. More permanent wooden structures, though, were underway. Lubbock put down $250 for a lot and another $250 to have a rude, one-room store constructed, with an attached shed at the back for sleeping quarters. For a long time, Lubbock recalled, there was little in the way of significant construction done, as there was (contrary to the Allens' claims) no good source of stone and too little labor available to cut lumber by hand in the absence of a sawmill. The most substantial residence in the new town was a log cabin, occupied by another of the Allen brothers, Henry, who had come to Texas to join his elder siblings in their new enterprise.[38]

Practical difficulties aside, Houston was off and running. By April, an enterprising theatrical producer named Lyons, describing himself as "being well acquainted with the Drama in all its forms," was seeking subscribers to fund the construction of a "well-regulated Theater, [which] is always a benefit to any community." Contributors would receive a season ticket to the new facility upon its completion. Another entrepreneur announced the issuance of shares in the new Texas Railroad, Navigation and Banking Company at Houston.[39] Even the *Telegraph and Texas Register* got caught up in the excitement and determined to move its press from Columbia (now West Columbia), on the Brazos River, to Houston, where the new capital would be established. The distance was only about fifty miles overland, but the difficulty of hauling the presses, type cabinets and other furnishings across the open countryside was daunting, so the staff loaded it all aboard the steamboat *Yellow Stone*, along with the growing archives of the new government, expecting an easier trip.[40] It didn't turn out that way:

> We left Columbia on the 16th ult. [April] in the steamer Yellow Stone, expecting that we should be able to issue this number of the Telegraph in the course of the same week, but disappointment and delay have met us at every turn. At Velasco [at the mouth of the Brazos] we [were] detained a week on account of the surf upon the bar; the tide left us fast aground one day at Clopper's bar and prevented us from reaching Lynchburg until the evening of the 26th, and a great part of the ensuing day was spent groping (if a steamboat can grope) at the rapid rate of one or two miles an hour, to the very crown of the "head of navigation of Buffalo Bayou" at the City of Houston.[41]

Perhaps stung a little by such accounts, it was inevitable that the Allens would attempt to disprove the criticism by bringing a bigger boat up the bayou. In May 1837, John Allen offered the master of the Sloo & Byrne steamboat *Constitution*, then lying at Galveston, $1,000 to bring his vessel to the foot of Houston's Main Street. Contrary to some accounts, *Constitution* was not a blue-water steamship by design. She was a riverboat, but a big one. *Constitution* had been built in Cincinnati in 1829, but at 150 feet long and 262 registered tons, she was one of the larger riverboats of her day and

> FOR SALE.
> If applied for immediately, The steam
> boat **Constitution,** as she now lies
> on the ways at our ship yard, on a liberal credit for approved apper.
>   HARROD & HUGHES
> m31 3t

Advertisement for the sale of Captain Auld's steamboat *Constitution*, from 1838. *From Huber's Advertisements of Lower Mississippi River Steamboats.*

four times the size of *Laura*. She was relatively deep-hulled, too, with a depth of hold of 7 feet 7 inches. In the spring of 1837, *Constitution* and her master, Edward Auld, were earning their way plying regularly between Galveston and New Orleans.[42]

Captain Auld was a seasoned mariner, though much of his experience was in blue water and under sail. He had voyaged out of Baltimore to ports as far as Kingston, Jamaica, and Rio de Janeiro.[43] Auld agreed to Allen's proposal and managed to reach Harrisburg with little difficulty. As with the little steamer *Laura* months before, though, he found it a long and difficult struggle to reach Allen's town site. It was a discouraging effort, but the boat's passengers attempted to put the best possible face on it by publishing an open letter of appreciation to Captain Auld,

> *expressing their grateful feelings for your kind and gentlemanly deportment, their high personal regard, and their respect for you as a commander. Under circumstances of great difficulty and some danger, you have made the first successful trip with a steamboat of this class from New Orleans to the capital of this republic, and this happy result is attributable to your skill, fortitude and persevering industry.*[44]

Captain Auld undoubtedly appreciated the sentiment (and presumably collected his cash), but he must also have discovered his problems were just beginning—at 150 feet from stempost to sternpost, with a bit more overhanging at either end, *Constitution* was simply too big to turn in the bayou at the Houston landing. In the end, Captain Auld was forced to reverse his big steamboat back down the bayou most of the way to Harrisburg, six-and-a-half miles, until he came to a spot where the waterway was sufficiently wide enough for him to swing the bow around and continue downstream normally.

Captain Auld never made another attempt to reach the Main Street landing. He continued running *Constitution* monthly between Galveston and New Orleans, though, and encountered enough hazards in so doing. In January 1838, he and *Constitution* were nearly wrecked on the Louisiana shore just east of Sabine Pass, but Auld and his crew managed to bring the crippled steamer safely into Galveston, albeit "in a damaged condition."[45] In fact, he eventually got out of running steamboats altogether and returned to sailing coasting schooners. He would be shipwrecked again in the fall of 1839 when his schooner, *Louisiana*, en route from Matagorda with a small cargo of tobacco, was driven ashore in a gale on an isolated part of the Louisiana coast. Captain Auld, his two crew members and three passengers survived but spent the next five weeks making their way through "bayou La Fourche, swamps & c., having been exposed eight days in an open boat, during which time they have traveled nearly three hundred miles—a large portion of the time tugging at the oar."[46]

Captain Auld's attempt to bring *Constitution* up to the Houston landing was not much of a success, but he did make a bit of Houston history in a way neither he nor the Allens intended; the spot where he finally managed to turn his boat around was soon dubbed *Constitution* Bend, in snarky remembrance of that embarrassing event. (See Buffalo Bayou and Galveston Bay Map, Event 1).[47]

Despite the difficulties they had to overcome, boats like *Laura*, *Yellow Stone* and *Constitution* had established that navigation of the bayou all the way up to the new town site at Houston was, in fact, feasible. Other boats and operators soon followed. *Laura* became a regular in the trade for a while, along with *Leonidas* (Captain Hanna) and *Branch T. Archer* (John E. Ross, master). *Archer*'s owners advertised her to make two round trips between Houston and Galveston each week; the fare for a passage aboard *Leonidas* was seven dollars. Later these were joined by *Sam Houston*, *Correo* and *Friend*.[48] When the steamer *Warsaw* arrived at Houston on her inaugural trip in July 1838, her passengers took out an advertisement thanking the boat's master, F.G. Lawrence, and pilot, James B. Wells, "for having performed the trip without any difficulty whatsoever." They went on to recommend the boat and her "superior accommodations, particularly for ladies."[49]

Competition for passengers was fierce from the beginning, and a common method for attracting customers was to tout a boat's speed. One of the earliest masters to make such a claim was Captain A.J. Davis, who advertised in 1838 that his new steamer, *San Jacinto*, would make three round trips between Galveston and Houston each week—one more than was then standard—and that *San Jacinto* had made a record passage between the two cities in just six hours. This last claim seems unlikely, though not impossible.[50]

Fares for passage and freight varied greatly, depending on the value of the currency in circulation. In August 1837, the going fare seems to have been about seven dollars.[51] But that was at a time when specie was sparse, and U.S. notes were the only currency in circulation. As new Republic of Texas currency began appearing, fares ballooned to ten dollars by January 1838[52] and to fifteen dollars by the end of 1838.[53] It caused enough of a concern among the public that four steamboat owners/masters—Davis of *San Jacinto*, John O'Brian of *Sam Houston*, John Selden of *Correo* and John Wheeler of *Friend*—formed a temporary cartel to standardize fares. They also bought advertising space to explain the higher rates. "Since the issue of promissory notes by the [Republic of Texas] government," they wrote, "the currency of the [United] States has entirely disappeared…It is unnecessary here to draw the too well known comparison as to the value of the two currencies." After giving a long list of their own expenses that had doubled in the inflationary spiral, the four captains announced their new fares at fifteen dollars for cabin passage, seven dollars and fifty cents on deck and similar increases for various categories of cargo.[54]

The natural hazards of the bayou remained a challenge, though, as did the open waters of Galveston Bay. It was common, for example, for boats throughout the era of the packets to get outside the channel at Clopper's Bar or Red Fish Bar; the one advantage there was that usually the boat would float free on the next tide. Just such a circumstance happened to Gustav Dresel, a German chronicler who traveled from Galveston to Houston aboard *Correo* in August 1838. The boat grounded hard on Clopper's Bar (See Buffalo Bayou and Galveston Bay Map, Event 2), and the passengers and crew were only able to get her off the following day after transferring all her cargo and baggage to boats and improvised rafts. Despite the discomfort, Dresel observed that the trip up the bayou was uniquely pleasant, with both banks densely covered with brush. The bayou itself, he noted, "becomes so canal-like that two boats are able to make way for each other in only a few places. Overhanging branches often brush the boat's deck…From among them is wafted the fragrance of the blossoms of the magnificent magnolia, which I have seen nowhere in such splendor and profusion." After passing the battlefield at San Jacinto, which Dresel noted was still littered with the

The Galveston–Houston Packet

A European depiction of Galveston in the 1840s. *Library of Congress.*

remains of the Mexican soldiers slaughtered there two years before, the *Correo* arrived in Houston at nine in the evening, after a journey of nearly thirty-six hours.[55]

Despite such difficulties, though, by the end of the decade, the steamboat trade envisioned by the Allens in the fall of 1836 seemed on pace to become a reality. Multiple boats were running regular schedules between Galveston and Houston, sparking rapid growth of both new cities. At least one boat was running each way, every day, and most were making two or even three round trips weekly. In the coming years, the constant traffic between Houston, which the Allens had argued would become "the great commercial emporium of Texas," and Galveston, which they predicted to be the "great naval and commercial depot of the country," looked to be the means by which those predictions would come about.[56]

Chapter 3

GONE TO TEXAS

The trees and shrubs grew to a prodigious height, and often met over the steamer, as she wound through the short reaches of this most lovely stream.
—Matilda Charlotte Houstoun, describing Buffalo Bayou in the 1840s

In these early days of the Texas Republic, and even going back to the days of Anglo-American immigration into Mexican Texas, the new territory was a frontier for people leaving one or another unpleasantness behind them in the United States. Creditors, jealous husbands, sticky legal entanglements—all of these could be avoided by quickly packing up and moving across the Sabine River into Texas, where the new immigrants would be safely beyond the reach of American law. The practice was so common that a sort of shorthand is supposed to have developed, whereby families would leave a parting message behind by scrawling on their doors the letters G.T.T.—"Gone to Texas."

One such man who relocated to Texas was John H. Sterrett, who had been a steamboat master on the Ohio River. Sterrett was born in Pennsylvania around 1815. Little is known about his early years, but by 1838, while still in his early twenties, Sterrett was master of a little sidewheel boat called *Rufus Putnam*, after the Revolutionary War general who had been a key player in the settlement of Ohio. Sterrett's boat was small, at 98 tons and 127 feet long, just slightly larger than *Laura* had been. The boat had been built in Marietta, Ohio, in 1835, but like many boats on the Ohio River, was formally registered at Pittsburgh.[57]

Sterrett's decision to leave the upper Ohio waterways and try his luck in Texas seems to have been prompted by an incident in Warsaw, Kentucky, sometime in the winter of 1837–38. Sterrett's original account of the incident does not survive, but he wrote about it to his sister, Juliet Sterrett Manlove, who in turn retold the story in a letter to their aunt. *Rufus Putnam*, with Sterrett as master, had loaded cargo at Cincinnati and then dropped about fifty miles down the Ohio River to Warsaw, on the stream's south bank. There they took on more cargo, along with a family moving to Arkansas. The family had a large quantity of furniture and household goods, and another member of the family, along with his African American slave, had accompanied them to the landing to help load it all on board. It was early in the morning, before sunup, when all was ready, and Sterrett prepared to get underway. He called for the family member on the bank to cast off the line securing the boat to the landing, but the man refused, demanding that Sterrett pay him for the labor of his slave in carrying the family's furnishings and loading them on the boat. Sterrett refused, stating plainly that the boat hadn't employed the black man in the first place and so was under no obligation to reimburse his owner for anything. They argued back and forth until Sterrett, wanting to be done with the whole business and on his way, instructed his boat's mate to have two hands go ashore in the steamboat's yawl to cast off the line themselves. Seeing this, the man on the bank swore that "he would shoot or kill the first man that would come on shore." No sooner had the crewmen reached the landing than the man attacked them. One of the crewmen shouted "Murder!" and a pistol shot cracked from somewhere on the steamboat. The man on the bank dropped instantly, apparently killed. The steamboat's crewmen hurriedly cast off the line and scrambled their way back to the boat, which quickly disappeared into the dark, steaming rapidly downstream in the direction of Louisville.[58]

Sterrett claimed he had neither fired the fatal shot nor knew who did. But he had no interest in getting caught up in an investigation of the incident and feared that "friends of the deceased would no doubt give him a good deal of trouble and perhaps cost him 2 or 3 thousand dollars as the Capt is held responsible for every thing that is done on board his boat." Captain Sterrett, his sister wrote, "has since gone over to Texas. There is but few [who] know it [and] if Inquesters should call to see you please [do] not tell them where John is as we think best to say nothing about it. Brother is very much hurt about it, but I hope it is all for his own good."[59]

John Sterrett did not give up immediately on the United States, for he maintained *Rufus Putnam*'s enrollment at Pittsburgh into the fall of 1838 and then just before Christmas that year filed a temporary registration for the

Steamboats on Buffalo Bayou

boat at New Orleans.⁶⁰ By January 1839, though, Sterrett and *Rufus Putnam* had crossed through the Gulf of Mexico and arrived at Galveston, where Sterrett announced his boat's availability for the Buffalo Bayou trade. Safety was clearly Sterrett's selling point to the general public. "This boat has lately been inspected and passed in the U.S. according to law, and is provided in case of fire with chain wheel ropes, an advantage not possessed by any other boat in the trade." Almost as an afterthought, Sterrett added, "Her accommodations for passengers are very extensive and superior."⁶¹ John Sterrett had "gone to Texas" and over the next forty years would become a vital, central figure in the developing steamboat trade between Galveston and Houston.

Captain Sterrett worked hard to make his name and his boat known. When he learned that a competing boat, *Emblem* (Captain Bryan), had made the trip up the bayou in eight hours, Sterrett pushed *Putnam* through a gale to Houston in less than seven.⁶²

In the early years of traffic on the bayou, the boats had run during the day. This was the preferred method and undoubtedly the safer approach, given the number of snags and sandbars in the stream. By the early 1840s, though, the standard method of operation was for most boats to leave either the Galveston or Houston terminals around five or six o'clock in the evening. In November 1841, one of the newer boats in the trade, *Victoria*, inaugurated a nighttime run. Undoubtedly *Victoria*'s master, John Delesdernier, recognized the value of making the trip at night and thus allowing his passengers a full day's business at each end of the trip. Delesdernier's competitors soon

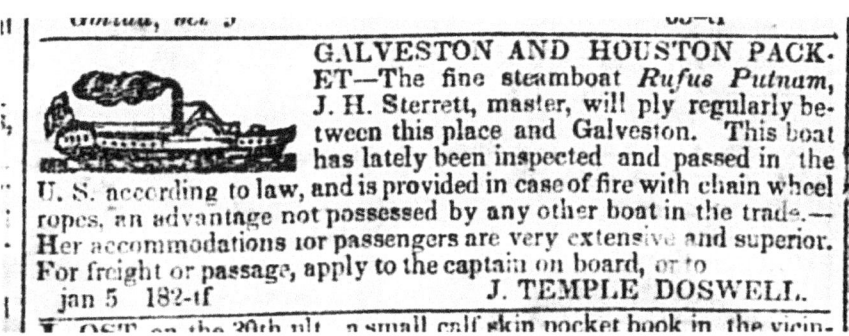

Advertisement for John H. Sterrett's boat *Rufus Putnam*, 1839. From the *Telegraph & Texas Register*.

followed suit, and until the end of the era, most boats on the run made their trips at night.⁶³

Perhaps the most vivid and complete account of steamboat travel on Buffalo Bayou during these early days comes from the travelogue of a young Englishwoman, Matilda Charlotte Houstoun (1815–1892). In the late summer of 1842, Houstoun (pronounced "Haweston") set out from London in the sailing yacht *Dolphin* to make a tour of the Gulf of Mexico. She was the daughter of naturalist Edward Jesse, who had obtained a sinecure in the Royal Household as the ceremonial "Gentleman of the Ewery," an "absurd and useless office" that nonetheless provided him an income of £300 per year, in addition to other perquisites. Jesse went on to hold a series of similar titles, through his friendship with the Duke of Clarence, who eventually succeeded to the throne as William IV (reigned 1830–37).⁶⁴

So it was that Jesse's daughter, Matilda, grew up on the privileged fringe of the British monarchy—a commoner, perhaps, but an extremely well-connected one. While still in her teens, she married the son of the British ambassador to the Kingdom of Saxony, but he died within a year, and she returned to live at the family home near Bushy Park in London. She subsequently married Captain M.C. Houstoun of the Tenth Hussars, a British cavalry regiment, and together they set out in *Dolphin* to begin an extensive tour of the Gulf of Mexico.⁶⁵ Captain Houstoun was interested in promoting a business venture involving a new device for packing and preserving beef, which involved injecting the veins and arteries of the carcass with saline;⁶⁶ his wife would devote her time recording her observations of life in the new republic. Matilda Charlotte Houstoun would later become one of the most successful female English novelists of the nineteenth century, but in the early 1840s, she was still an unknown writer, compiling a travelogue that she would publish under the name "Mrs. Houstoun."

Shortly before Christmas 1842, *Dolphin* and the Houstouns arrived at Galveston. Mrs. Houstoun was not impressed. It was a town that

> *gives one, on a first view, no very high idea of its importance. The houses in general are small, though, here and there, an overgrown rickety-looking building speaks of the larger means and higher pretensions of its occupant… It is strange, that here, where bricks could so easily be made, the inhabitants should still continue satisfied with their wooden tenements. The only bricks I saw in Galveston were those forming one solitary chimney. It is calculated that, on an average, these wooden houses last ten years; and in the mean time they are very liable to be blown down…*

Steamboats on Buffalo Bayou

Galveston as depicted in Mrs. Houstoun's travelogue in the 1840s. From Houstoun's *Texas and the Gulf of Mexico.*

> *The city contains about three hundred covered buildings, which a bold person would, or might call houses. There are also four churches; rather a considerable proportion, I should say to the number of inhabitants, which amount only to about two thousand. Then, there are temples, squares, theatres, botanical and zoological gardens; but they are only at present on the ground plan.*[67]

The Houstouns remained in Galveston only for a month or so and didn't venture far into the interior. In late January 1843, they sailed for New Orleans and spent the next few weeks exploring the Crescent City. They then returned to Galveston and, on a "bright, frosty day," boarded the steamboat *Dayton*, Captain D.S. Kelsey, for Houston.[68] *Dayton* was a Pittsburgh-built boat that, having been launched some eight years before, was getting a little long in the tooth. At 111 tons, *Dayton* was a bit larger than Sterrett's *Rufus Putnam*. Nonetheless, Houstoun found the boat crowded and spent a good deal of her time aboard on the boat's hurricane deck, despite the cold. There she encountered a string of male passengers who would politely inquire, "Do you liquor, ma'am?" and offer a flask of "egg-noggy." Houstoun must have accepted the offer at least once, for she confessed about the potable, "I cannot deny its excellence."[69]

THE GALVESTON–HOUSTON PACKET

An 1850s caricature of steamboat table manners. *Harper's Magazine.*

Soon after departure, the midday meal was served, and Houstoun found all to be "very orderly and civil." The female cabin passengers remained quiet during the meal, in contrast to their behavior in their own salon, which Houstoun described as "deafening." The main courses consisted of alternating plates of boiled oysters and freshly butchered steaks, neither of which Houstoun found to her liking. Later that day, the evening meal was delayed for a time while the boat landed and the cook went ashore to shoot and butcher another beef.[70]

After supper, Houstoun returned to the top of the boat to discover that they had entered Buffalo Bayou proper. The low, swampy marsh on either side gave way to high, heavily wooded banks. Despite the winter season, Houstoun saw magnolia trees she estimated to be eighty feet in height, along with firs, laurels and cistus covering the ground. "It seemed one vast shrubbery," she wrote. "The trees and shrubs grew to a prodigious height, and often met over the steamer, as she wound through the short reaches of this most lovely stream." Houstoun also made note of the singing of African American slaves aboard the boat, "carolling out their nightly songs [which were] the most dismal and unearthly. They were seated, some on the hurricane deck and others at their work, but all joining in the same loud, weary, monotonous chaunt."[71]

Eventually Houstoun retired to her cabin, which opened onto the main salon where the men were and was separated from it by only a lightweight, louvered door. By this time, the ladies had returned to their salon, while the men remained in the main salon. Drinking and card playing were the main pastimes in both places, with the addition of chewing tobacco in the main cabin. In her cabin, Houstoun listened to the men's conversations:

> *Their talk as usual was of dollars: politics, indeed, occasionally took their turn, but the subject ceased to become interesting, when the pockets of the company could no longer be affected by the turn of affairs. There was no private scandal, no wit, no literature, no small talk; all was hard, dry, calculating business. I heard many shrewd hard-headed remarks; the fate of their country was talked over as a matter of business, and one rather important looking gentleman made a stump speech on the expediency of Texas becoming a colony of Great Britain!*[72]

Dayton arrived at the landing at Houston at seven o'clock the following morning, having made the passage in seventeen hours—probably a very typical time for those early days. The Houstouns had hoped to travel farther into the interior, perhaps as far as Washington, former capital of the republic and near the head of navigation on the Brazos River. The weather remained unseasonably cold, though, into the spring, and eventually the English couple abandoned their plans for further travel inland. The dogwood trees had blossomed but, Matilda Houstoun noted, "the thermometer was four degrees below freezing point."[73] Somewhat reluctantly, they re-boarded Captain Kelsey's *Dayton* for the return trip to Galveston, where their yacht *Dolphin* awaited them.

On this occasion they set out in the morning, affording the boat's passengers a daytime view of the waterway. As before, Houstoun remained on the hurricane deck in spite of the cold, noting the sharp turns in the bayou and that the boat frequently touched the bank. She herself was in some danger, she discovered, receiving a "pretty sharp blow" from the branch of a tree that overhung the boat.[74] Breakfast was served on board, consisting of beef, raw eggs and "the infallible egg noggy, [which] was drank both by ladies and gentlemen."[75] Houstoun spent the rest of the morning in the ladies' salon aft, where Mrs. Kelsey insisted on giving her a knitting lesson.

Dinner, the midday meal, was a roast pig and parsnips that was "as usual, dispatched in an incredibly short space of time." After the meal it was announced that as the result of a norther—a high, steady, north wind that lasted for several days—much of the water had been blown out of Galveston Bay. The water level was so low at Clopper's Bar that the boat could not pass, and they were obliged to tie up at Morgan's Point until the water rose again. The passengers went ashore and occupied their time in various ways; Captain Houstoun managed to shoot a possum, which was a novel creature to him. It was an object of brief curiosity until other passengers, more familiar with the fauna of Texas, appropriated it for the cook with the assurance that the animal was "first rate eating."[76]

On the morning of the third day, they finally got underway again, only to be delayed once more, within sight of Galveston, by a mechanical casualty to the boat's engine. They finally reached the wharf at Galveston late that evening, sixty hours or more after setting out from Houston. By this time, any rustic charm *Dayton* might have had for Matilda Houstoun must have worn very thin, for she referred to the boat as the "dirty little steamer" in comparison to her personal yacht, with its holystoned decks, polished guns and bright paintwork, which she considered "a perfect luxury to the sight."[77]

Delays like those experienced by the Houstouns aboard *Dayton* were important for reasons other than passengers' convenience. With the establishment of regular packet service between Galveston and Houston, steamboat owners began to jostle for contracts for carrying the mail, which had proved to be critical in subsidizing early steamboat service on the Ohio and Mississippi. Mail contracts provided a powerful incentive for operators to provide regular and reliable service between cities, specifying regular schedules and punctual delivery. Steamboat operators who failed to meet these standards faced penalties for non-performance or, if problems persisted, loss of the contract altogether. Mail contracts were also good for attracting regular business; they were prominently advertised by steamboat owners as a sort of official government endorsement of the boat, with the letters U.S.M., for United States Mail, emblazoned on the paddlewheel boxes. While the income from a mail contract could not keep a steamboat in operation by itself, it could add significantly to the boat's bottom line and often determined whether the ink in the clerk's ledger was mostly red or black.[78]

The Republic of Texas Congress passed an act in February 1840 authorizing the postmaster general to contract for the transport of mail between Galveston and Houston at least twice each week. In actual practice, though, prompt delivery was often more problematic. One Houston resident recorded the annoyance of having "the United States mail lay at Galveston two days after its arrival, to have it put on board the slowest boat that runs on the bayou and to have that boat lay three days on Red Fish Bar."[79]

By January 1844, some months after the Houstouns' trips aboard *Dayton* with Captain Kelsey, John Sterrett took over the boat. In the fall, Sterrett's *Dayton* would carry from Galveston to Houston more than fifty returned Texian prisoners from the Mier Expedition (1842–43), men who had been captured by the Mexican army while raiding Mexican settlements along the disputed border territory between the two countries. In what would become known in Texas lore as the "Black Bean Incident," the prisoners had infamously been forced to draw black or white beans from a pot to determine which would be shot in retribution. Seventeen men were subsequently executed; most of the others were eventually released and made their way home, some of them aboard *Dayton*.[80]

In the fall of 1845, Texas voters formally adopted an ordinance annexing their republic to the United States. It was a move that, many hoped, would provide both security and stability to the region's rough-and-tumble experience as an independent republic. During that same decade, the Galveston–Houston packet trade had followed a similar course. By trial and error, it had gradually become a regular and profitable enterprise. Captains like Sterrett and Kelsey and Auld of the old *Constitution* had sorted out the peculiarities of navigation on Galveston Bay, San Jacinto Bay and Buffalo Bayou and had gradually settled into an operational routine that—occasional groundings notwithstanding—would become standard for decades to come. They set the stage for the following decade, when they and their boats would fully come into their own, a sort of "golden age" of steam navigation on the bayou.

Chapter 4

YEARS OF GROWTH AND STABILITY

Comfort, economy and speed
—*Motto of the Houston Navigation Company, in the 1850s.*

By the time Texas entered the Union in the last days of 1845, the Buffalo Bayou trade was well established and settled into a routine that would carry it through the next three decades. The boats were generally running at night; the supporting infrastructure of agents, wharves and warehouses had been established at both Galveston and Houston. Passages through Red Fish Bar and Clopper's Bar had been cut, and getting temporarily stranded on one or the other, to await a rising tide, was becoming a rare event. The days of experimentation and trial-and-error were past, and the steamboatmen on Buffalo Bayou now entered a period marked by growth, competition and consolidation. The years between annexation and the coming of the Civil War would become, in retrospect, the golden age of the Galveston–Houston packet trade.

Seeing the possibilities for continued growth of the packet trade between Galveston and Houston, a group of Houston businessmen moved in 1851 to consolidate their resources into a single company to dominate the market. Led by merchant William Marsh Rice, the limited partnership organized itself as the Houston and Galveston Navigation Company. Rice's share in the venture was $5,000; twenty-five other merchants, businessmen and pilots contributed between $250 and $2,000 for places as special partners. John Sterrett, who would soon rise to be superintendent of the growing fleet, went in for $1,000.[81]

The Galveston–Houston Packet

Perhaps the best-known aspect of steamboat travel on the Western Rivers in these years was racing. Usually these were impromptu heats, informally undertaken when the opportunity arose. Racing is mentioned so often in travelers' accounts of the period that one might guess it was an occurrence on every passage. That was never the case, although it did happen often enough, because there were real incentives to engage in the practice. With two boats traveling the same route and stopping at the same landings, the first boat to arrive would be able to take on the lion's share of the freight and passengers waiting there to board. Winning a race against an established, respected boat on a certain route was a common way for a new boat and her master to make a name for themselves and raise their visibility among the traveling public. Finally, the passengers themselves often encouraged the practice, looking for something exciting to occupy the long hours of a passage.[82]

Part of the thrill of a steamboat race, at least for some passengers, was the risk of spectacular death and dismemberment in a resulting boiler explosion. Steamboat racing was irrevocably associated with such disasters in the public mind, and there were many, many anecdotal examples in evidence. Newspaper editors issued frequent warnings against the folly of racing—a sure sign that the boats were doing just that—and, as one chronicler of Buffalo Bayou's early years observed, "in every instance when a boiler blew up, another boat was very near."[83] But that view was hardly unanimous; years after his own days on the river, Mark Twain would scoff at such fears, arguing that

> *the public always had an idea that racing was dangerous; whereas the opposite was the case—that is, after the laws were passed which restricted each boat to just so many pounds of steam to the square inch. No engineer was ever sleepy or careless when his heart was in a race. He was constantly on the alert, trying gauge-cocks and watching things. The dangerous place was on slow, plodding boats, where the engineers drowsed around and allowed chips to get into the "doctor"* [i.e., a feed pump] *and shut off the water supply from the boilers.*[84]

It's difficult to estimate the amount of racing that took place on the Houston-Galveston route. It was rare that pilots or crews publicly acknowledged that races occurred, and given the common view of racing

Steamboats on Buffalo Bayou

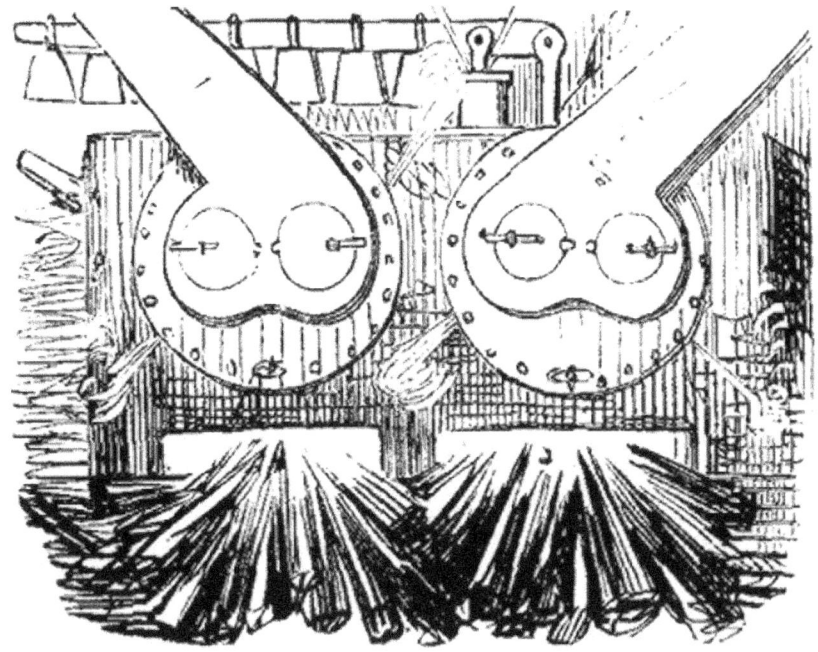

Caricature of a racing steamboat, the fireboxes stuffed with fuel and the safety valves clamped down. *Harper's Magazine.*

as a "criminally reckless" pastime, their reticence is perhaps understandable. But the reputation of a boat or master could be made in such an encounter, and the inevitable temptation to pit one boat against another must have been the cause of many a contest.

One of the earliest races on Galveston Bay occurred in May 1848, between the steamboats *Billow*, bound for the Trinity River, and *McLean*, headed up Buffalo Bayou. *McLean* cast off first from the Galveston wharf at about ten in the morning on May 27; *Billow* followed fifteen minutes later, "dashing after her as if she had complete mastery of the billows on which she bounded like a sea bird." Witnesses saw dense plumes of black smoke issue from *Billow*'s chimneys, suggesting a large quantity of pitch and pine knots cast into her furnaces, and for a time, *Billow* seemed to be gaining on *McLean*. Then *McLean*'s engineer began tossing his own pitch into that boat's furnaces, and the race was on in earnest. "Both boats now dashed over the water like things of life, and broad ridges of white foam streamed at their bows and along their sides…Thus they ran 'nip and tuck' as the boatmen style it, until they reached Red Fish Bar, where they parted, the

Billow going to the mouth of the Trinity and *McLean* to Houston. The trip from Galveston to the Bar, a distance of twenty miles, was accomplished in an hour and twenty minutes."[85]

Not all such races ended happily, though. The most notorious incident in the history of the packets, and one of the deadliest maritime disasters in Texas history, began as just such a race. In the winter of 1852–53, John Sterrett, now master of the Pennsylvania-built sternwheeler *Neptune*, developed an intense rivalry with Captain Webb of the sidewheeler *Farmer*. Two years previously, before joining the Houston and Galveston Navigation Company, Sterrett himself had been master of *Farmer*.[86] Both vessels were considered "crack" boats. The men pitted their boats against one another, and on one run to Galveston in January, the two boats actually came in contact with one another. No one was hurt, but that race set the stage for another one two months later. Early on the morning of March 22, 1853, the boats were again racing to Galveston when, a few miles from the finish, *Farmer*'s boiler burst (See Buffalo Bayou and Galveston Bay Map, Event 3). The explosion demolished the boiler and hurricane decks above and blasted dozens of passengers and crew into the water. Captain Sterrett turned *Neptune* around to render assistance, but for many of those in the water, it was too late. Of about seventy-two persons on board *Farmer*, at least thirty-six were killed. Captain Webb was among the dead. The steamer's mate, Curtis Blakeman, and pilot, Michael McCormick, were injured; both would later rise to become two of the best-known and popular pilots on the route. Also among the injured was passenger Sidney Sherman, a hero of the Battle of San Jacinto who would soon thereafter begin working to establish Texas' first railroad.[87]

The papers lauded Captain Sterrett's efforts to save the passengers and crew of *Farmer*, but they also criticized both him and Captain Webb for behaving with criminal recklessness in racing their boats in the first place. It was reported that, even at the moment of the explosion, one of the passengers had been arguing with Captain Webb against the competition, and that this same gentleman had circulated a written protest among the passengers to present to the captain.[88] The surviving officers were never charged, but the incident lingered in the minds of fare-paying passengers and brought about changes in the way the boats were run. After the accident, the boats under Sterrett's direction were said to have established a reputation for safety and comfort.[89]

The detailed casualty lists published after the accident give a useful insight as to how at least some of the boats' crews were organized. According to

Contemporary illustration of the *Farmer* explosion. The vessels here are shown incorrectly as coastal steamers, not riverboats, but the violence of the image is accurate. *Author's collection.*

press accounts, *Farmer* carried a crew of twenty-seven. Of those, eight are identified by name and task (pilot, clerk, carpenter, etc.). Of the remaining nineteen crewmen listed—most of whom must have been firemen, stewards and deckhands—eleven were African American slaves belonging to people not directly connected to the *Farmer* or her owners. It was commonplace for slaveowners along the Lower Mississippi to hire out their slaves to work on the river, and the casualty list of the *Farmer* suggests that the practice was carried over into Texas. Several years after the disaster, the

Advertisements.

Galveston and Houston Steam Packet NEPTUNE.
JOHN H. STERRETT, Master.

THIS splendid new passenger Steamer, built expressly for this trade, has been running in it six months, and been able to sustain herself, notwithstanding the fierce opposition waged, for which the owners acknowledge their indebtedness, mainly to support derived from the travelling community, return their sincere thanks and beg to inform and assure the public, that she will continue to run in the trade, " and no mistake," and that, too, as an *independent* boat.

During the summer months, she will leave Houston every Wednesday and Saturday, at 3 o'clock, p. m., and Galveston, every Tuesday and Friday evening at three o'clock, making her time through generally in about seven hours.

Rate of passage, two dollars, as fixed on her first trip, *which will not be deviated from.*

B. A. SHEPHERD,
Managing owner.

Houston, May 28, 1853.   46-6m

Advertisement for John H. Sterrett's *Neptune*, several weeks after the *Farmer* disaster. From the *Telegraph & Texas Register.*

prevailing rate for slaves to work as deckhands on the Houston-Galveston run was $480 per year—paid to their owner, of course. Two other *Farmer* crewmen are listed as "German" and were probably recent immigrants from Europe.[90]

There were other accidents, as well. One of the worst of these occurred when the nearly new steamer *Bayou City* blew up her boilers around one o'clock on the morning of September 28, 1860, while making the passage up Buffalo Bayou from Galveston.[91] The boilers had failed along their bottom surface, the blast wrecking the deck beneath them. The boilers themselves went the other way, crashing up through the main salon and cabins above, before falling back down into the hull of the boat. Following them down into the cloud of scalding steam and water came smashed cabin paneling, furniture, bedding, luggage, crockery, at least one passenger and the boat's

Grave of two victims of the *Farmer* explosion, Thomas Pritchard and Anthony Dunlevy, Galveston. *Author's photo.*

master. Passenger Thomas Westrop "had fallen in among the boilers, and died soon after being raised." Captain James Forrest, who had been on the upper deck of the boat, was dropped down into the wreckage as well but managed to extricate himself with only minor injuries. There were at least ten dead, including Isaiah Irvin, Speaker of the Georgia House of Representatives, and two African American men among the crew who were property of Captain Forrest.[92]

The local U.S. Steamboat Inspectors, Captain James Haviland and Israel Clark, eventually determined that the explosion had occurred due to a buildup of salt and scale inside one of the boilers. This was a particular problem for boats running between Houston and Galveston, for, unlike boats on the Mississippi and Ohio Rivers, the Texas boats spent much of their operating lives in salt water, which was used in the boilers. The scale prevented efficient transfer of the heat from the furnaces into the water inside the boiler. As a result, the iron boilerplate absorbed most of the heat, becoming hotter—and consequently softer—until it failed catastrophically, with fatal results. The inspectors revoked the licenses of *Bayou City*'s two surviving engineers, Numa M. Whitson and John Curly, for "ignorance or neglect of duty" in not keeping the boilers properly clear of scale and allowing it "to accumulate on the boilers of that boat to such a degree as to cause the fatal explosion heretofore reported."[93]

With the inspectors' work completed, *Bayou City* was turned back to her owners. The repairs would be extensive; the entire forward half of the boat had been wrecked. It would be months before the boat would be ready again, but by then secession and civil war would overtake the normal operations of the steamboats running on the bayou. *Bayou City*'s life so far had been short and tragic, but the most dramatic chapter in the boat's life was yet to come.

The limited partnership formed by Rice, Sterrett and others in 1851 had run its charter by the beginning of 1854, and the partners reorganized the company under the name of the Houston Navigation Company. One priority for the newly reorganized company was to secure federal mail contracts. These contracts—essentially government subsidies for steamboat operators—dramatically expanded in the 1850s. Though the stringent requirements of postal contracts were difficult to meet, the cash payments that came with such contracts often made the difference between a steamboat line's profit and loss.

Steamboats on Buffalo Bayou

The U.S. Mail route through Galveston and Buffalo Bayou to Houston was a particularly important one and often at the center of controversy. Galveston was a primary terminal for one of the main transcontinental mail routes, one that began in New Orleans, went by coastal steamer to Galveston, then overland to San Antonio, El Paso, Santa Fe and points farther west, all the way to San Francisco—total contractual transit time from the Crescent City to Frisco was twenty-five days.[94]

Galveston, though, was seen by many as a problem and came to be known as a bottleneck in the fast and efficient transport of the mail. Galveston's monopoly on mail coming in from the rest of the United States was a source of deep annoyance for both citizens and newspapermen, who charged that publishers on the island were using their influence to hold newspapers coming in from other parts of the country for several days, allowing the Galveston publishers the ability to go to print first with the latest national news. This frustration led to many customers avoiding the U.S. Mails altogether, sending valuable parcels and shipments by way of one of the private express companies that sprang up to carry mail and valuable packages along their own routes, generally overland.

Controversy and competition from private carriers notwithstanding, the U.S. Mail remained a critical part of life and commerce in Texas, and almost all of it was routed through Galveston. It was largely one-way traffic, too. The postmaster there in the late 1850s, H.B. Andrews, reported that his post office handled about 150,000 pieces of incoming mail, much of which was sent on to the interior by way of Buffalo Bayou and other routes, while only handling about 30,000 pieces of outgoing mail.[95]

John Sterrett and Frederick Smith bid successfully for a $20,000 mail contract in 1858 that required them to provide mail service between Galveston and Houston six times per week. This was likely the largest single contract and route out of Galveston, including as it did not only mail destined for Harrisburg and Houston but also points north and west of the Bayou City. With the requirement for mail service six days every week, it was also the most regular and frequent. The Houston Navigation Company was well established by this time, so Sterrett and Smith likely had little trouble meeting the terms of the mail contract. Nonetheless, there were critics always ready to pounce, as when, just a few weeks after Sterrett and Smith won their contract, complaints were being made about Sterrett's failure to deliver the mail as expected. The *Galveston Civilian and Gazette* came to Sterrett's defense, pointing out that it was the first time in twenty years that he'd failed to carry the mails, and even in this case, it was a trip outside the

The Galveston–Houston Packet

Advertisement from the 1850s for the Houston Navigation Company's boats. *Houston Metropolitan Research Center.*

strict terms of his contract. Sterrett, the *Civilian and Gazette* pointed out, "has been running between Houston and Galveston nineteen years, and in that time has made four thousand trips between the two places. Every man who has ever travelled in Texas knows him, and very few who have ever made a trip with him but tell their friends to do the same thing. Justice requires us to say there are other boats in the Houston trade that will compare well with steamboats anywhere; but Capt. Sterrett always manages to command the best one."[96]

During this period, the late 1850s, the H.N.Co. ran three boats on a regular schedule between Houston and Galveston. Promising "comfort, economy and speed," the H.N.Co. offered daily service between the two cities. A schedule from about 1858 lists the new sidewheeler *Diana*, under Sterrett's command, leaving Galveston for Houston on Sunday and Thursday mornings; *Island City*, Captain Blakeman, ran the same route on Monday, Wednesday and Friday evenings. The old sternwheeler *Neptune*, soon to be replaced by a new sidewheeler of the same name, was kept in reserve. When the evening boats arrived in Houston after midnight, cabin passengers could disembark or remain on board "at pleasure until the leaving of the morning trains" for points farther inland. Cabin passage cost the traveler three dollars, a considerably lower fare than citizens of the Republic had paid just a few years before.[97]

The Houston Navigation Company completely dominated the steamboat trade between Galveston and Houston during this period. Though none of the other boats running on the bayou were able to successfully challenge the company for long, the steady competition from independent boats kept the H.N.Co.'s fares reasonable for both freight and passengers. When a new boat appeared to challenge the Houston Navigation Company, a quick, dramatic rate fight would follow. The H.N.Co., with its fleet of packets and its mail contract, invariably undercut the opponent's fares and forced the competitor out of business. During these brief periods, though, careful passengers could wrangle bargains out of the clerks on competing boats. The fares occasionally dropped as low as one dollar for cabin passage. One passenger in 1857 wrote that upon

> reaching Galveston we took a steamboat for Houston…Before the rate fight the fare had been $5. The dining tables were strung along the center of the cabin and every few feet there was a bucket of champagne on ice. If a man had the capacity he could drink $4 worth of champagne on his dollar ticket. The dining service was solid silver and there was a black man to hand you

The Galveston–Houston Packet

a match when you wanted to light a cigar. It was about as hospitable on the boat as in a southern planter's home.[98]

The ready availability of food and drink notwithstanding, the passage between Galveston and Houston could be a dull one. Bored passengers often turned to gambling to pass the time. Jim Parcell, who traveled the Buffalo Bayou route not long before the Civil War, recalled that one evening, after dinner, he and a friend met a cotton merchant from New Orleans who'd come to Texas on a buying trip. The merchant was bored and suggested a "little game." It would turn out to be an expensive proposition. Parcell noted that after a few hands

> *I had $400 of the New Orleans man's root of all evil, and was just getting interested, when he suddenly stopped, and fingered through his pockets. Then his face turned very red.*
>
> *"My friend," he said apologetically, "I thought I had some money, but it seems I misjudged my finances. It was very uncivil of me, and I must beg your pardon."*
>
> *He was actually very sorry because he had induced me to go into a game with him without having enough money to make it interesting. Suddenly the purser went by, and a happy smile spread over the face of my genteel antagonist.*
>
> *"Billy," he said, "I am a little—ah—shy of cash. Could you—ah"*
>
> *"Let you have a few hundred?" replied the purser genially. "How much do you want, Colonel?"*
>
> *"Could you make it, say, $500?"*
>
> *"To be sure—a thousand if you want it."*
>
> *The purser went to the safe and returned with a bundle of new bills which he slipped into the hands of the New Orleans man without ostentation. We resumed the game, and before we reached the landing, the genial colonel's $500 was lying alongside his $400 in my pocketbook, and we were the best of friends.*[99]

It's difficult to know the number of professional gamblers who plied their craft on the Galveston–Houston route, partly because victims would be reluctant to discuss their losses. In one case, at least, the gamblers operated as an organized team to relieve unsuspecting passengers of their cash. One foggy evening in February 1856, the Galveston-bound packet *Neptune* got out of the channel at Red Fish Bar and went aground. The packet would float free within a few hours on the next high tide, but in the meantime, the bored passengers gathered to amuse themselves with card games. Attention soon fell

> upon two or three well-dressed men, one of whom was proposing to take bets on a trick at cards, which looked very much, in principle, like thimble rig, while the others made occasional bets to decoy the green ones. One victim I noticed, went into the trap to the extent of a hundred dollars, and another paid twenty for his experience. The game is called three-card monte, and the players are frequent passengers between Galveston and Houston. During the passage is the best time to get up a game, which, in the vernacular peculiarly applied, is a "dead thing."[100]

There were less expensive pastimes, as well; Sterrett was said to have endeared himself to passengers by engaging in a friendly rivalry with the clerk of whichever boat he happened to be on, for the attention of the female passengers. Invariably each evening, there came a point where Sterrett would, with theatrical flourish, jokingly admonish the clerk to go below and "check your cotton, sir. I'm the ladies' man on this boat!" Over a span of nearly forty years, Sterrett must have used that gag a thousand times.[101]

While he played the "ladies' man" on his boats, Sterrett was very much spoken for and by this point had a growing family. Sterrett had married Susan Wilson, a woman eleven years his junior, in 1843 when he was twenty-eight and she in her late teens. Their first child, daughter Henrietta, was born in 1847, followed by additional siblings at regular intervals. By 1858, John and Susan had at least five children, with the prospect of more yet to come. They built a house in Houston on the corner of San Jacinto and McKinney Streets, in what is now the heart of downtown. A contemporary newspaper account described his new residence as "quite an addition to the appearance of that neighborhood." Sterrett probably needed the space for his growing family.[102]

The Houston Navigation Company maintained two offices. The Galveston office was located on Central Wharf, a long pier built out into the harbor from the head of Twenty-first Street. Central Wharf, also known as Morgan's Wharf, also housed the local agents for Charles Morgan's line of steamships. The Morgan Line, with its growing web of steamship routes, inland rivers packets and land transport, was already the dominating force in transportation on the Gulf of Mexico. The complementary operations of the Morgan Line and the Houston Navigation Company led to a close relationship between the businesses, which would later culminate in the Morgan Line's purchase of the packet company. The Houston office was located near the landing, on Commerce Street between Main and Fannin. Sterrett served as both the Houston agent and commodore of the company's fleet.

In the fifteen years between the annexation of Texas and the coming of the Civil War, the Buffalo Bayou packet trade entered its maturity and cemented its role in the expansion of development and commerce in Texas. For men like John Sterrett, they were good times; the late 1850s arguably marked the peak of the bayou trade, a time when it was largely unchallenged as a link between Texas' two premier cities and directly responsible for the booming expansion of both.

But even as the decade of the 1850s drew to a close, there were signs of change and challenge ahead. The railroad projects that dreamers had talked about for years were finally being built across the prairies; Charles Morgan, the New York shipping magnate, was aggressively moving forward with his consolidation of shipping in the Gulf of Mexico; and increased agitation between northern and southern states over the future of slavery in the territories to the west had some political leaders in the South talking openly about secession. If the decade of the 1850s had been one of steady growth and stability on Buffalo Bayou, the decade that followed would be one of upheaval, catastrophe and rebuilding.

Chapter 5

THE TEXAS MARINE DEPARTMENT

Our only chance is to get alongside before they hit us.
—Leon Smith, commander of the Confederate cottonclads at the Battle of
Galveston

The first casualty of the Civil War on Buffalo Bayou was an unnamed Confederate soldier who had the misfortune to be a recruit in a militia company organized by members of the local *turnverein*, a health and physical fitness movement that was popular among German immigrants to the United States. The company organized by the Houston *turnverein*, the Turner Rifles, was commanded by Captain E.B.H. Schneider, a thirty-one-year-old native Rhinelander.[103] Schneider was one of the founders of the Houston *turnverein* and, in keeping with the spirit of that organization, he drilled them strenuously. Schneider "at once sought to apply the most rigid discipline and exhaustive methods in training his men to be soldiers," one Houstonian would recall years later. The captain would load them down with camp equipment, packs, cartridge boxes and the like and march them far out into the countryside and back. He also liked to drill the men at quick time and double-quick, "for the amusement of people who had gathered to see them drill."[104]

If Captain Schneider was proud of his soldiers, though, he was also vain and, on one day, criminally stupid. One afternoon in early 1861, seeking to push his company into ever-more spectacular feats of military drill, he marched them down San Jacinto Street, across the wharf and into the bayou.

He evidently assumed they would continue marching in formation across the bottom, and emerge on the other bank "as if nothing had happened." It didn't work out that way, of course; there was an eight-foot drop into the bayou from the wharf and, thanks to ongoing dredging efforts, the water there was twelve or fifteen feet deep. Remarkably, only one of the soldiers drowned, a young man who to that point had been deemed the best all-around athlete and swimmer in the company. The body was recovered and laid out in the city armory; the dead man's rites were said to have been the first military funeral in Texas during the war.[105]

Texas' secession from the Union on February 1, 1861, was followed by a public referendum three weeks later to affirm the actions of the Secession Convention. The convention reconvened on March 2—chosen because it was the twenty-fifth anniversary of Texas' Declaration of Independence from Mexico during the Texas Revolution—to announce the results.[106] Texans voted overwhelmingly for secession, by a factor of roughly three-to-one; in Harris and Galveston counties, the fire-eaters supporting secession scored even bigger victories, with 88.3 percent and 95.9 percent of the vote, respectively.

The "secession winter" of 1860–61 coincided with the cotton season. The season looked to be a strong one, though probably not a record, with Galveston receiving a total of 66,853 bales of cotton during the first five months of 1861. Most of these came by boat, and most of those from steamboats plying Buffalo Bayou, the Trinity River and the Brazos.[107]

On April 19, 1861, days after the Confederacy opened fire on Fort Sumter in Charleston Harbor, President Lincoln declared a blockade of Confederate ports. The blockade was a key element in the Union's grand strategy, widely known as the Anaconda Plan, to surround the South and choke off its commerce and possible support from overseas. It extended from the Virginia Capes southward, around Florida and the Gulf of Mexico to the mouth of the Rio Grande. Like the South American constrictor for which it was named, the Anaconda Plan would gradually squeeze the life out of the rebellion. But it was a job far easier said than done; through a series of meetings that spring, the U.S. Navy's Blockade Strategy Board eventually came to realize the scope of the task at hand. Even so, as late as September 1861, the board still believed that an effective blockade of the Texas coast could be carried out by a total of four Union navy vessels, three at Galveston and one shallow-draft gunboat to sweep all the bays and inlets between Galveston and the Rio Grande.[108]

The blockade at Galveston began on July 2, with the arrival of USS *South Carolina*. Her commander, Captain James Alden, sent a boat into the harbor under a flag of truce, announcing the formal imposition of the blockade.[109] Alden soon seized several small sailing craft that he organized into a miniature flotilla, but the main success of his blockade during this period rested on other, larger factors. In the first place, the war was still new; when Alden arrived, the Battle of First Manassas/Bull Run, with its brutal introduction to large-scale combat, was still almost three weeks off. Many still believed, in that summer of 1861, that the conflict would be over within months, and few were willing to risk valuable ships and cargoes when they believed they could afford to sit out the conflict and resume their normal trade soon enough. Before the war, the "coastwise" trade between Galveston and other U.S. ports had accounted for just over half of the city's $12.9 million in exports;[110] those ports were now either closed to Southern shipping or blockaded themselves. Foreign shippers were reluctant to trade with the South, for fear of poisoning commerce relations with their more important trading partners in the North. Above all, there was reluctance on the part of the Confederacy to let *any* of its exports go, especially "King Cotton," on the assumption that the European powers' demand for the staple would eventually force them to intervene in the conflict, and break the Union blockade. It was wishful thinking, but it still seemed a plausible outcome in the summer of '61.

Commerce quickly ground to a halt. There were few vessels attempting to run the blockade—Galveston and Texas were too far removed from the center of the conflict—so most of the Buffalo Bayou packets sat idle while cotton remaining from the 1860–61 shipping season piled up in warehouses. U.S government subsidies for mail service, always a critical element in boat operators' financial calculations, evaporated. Within a few months, steamboat owners tried to recoup their losses by chartering or selling their boats to the Confederate government. In September 1861, the Houston Navigation Company offered three of its boats—*Diana*, *Bayou City* and *Neptune No. 2*—for charter or sale to the Confederate government:

The Galveston–Houston Packet

GALVESTON, September 23, 1861.

We (acting for the association known as the Houston Navigation Company) propose to charter to the Confederate States Government three of our steamers, viz, Diana, Bayou City, and Neptune No. 2, on the following terms:

(The Government assuming all risk of their loss arising from burning or capture by the enemy or by navigating in any waters more hazardous than voyages to Houston from Galveston by the usual route, rating the value to be paid for in case of loss of each boat at $25,000.)

For $7,500 per month for each boat—we furnishing them fuel and crew and provisions for crew—the charter to be for not less than one month and to continue for whole months if continued beyond one month, and in case of contemplated dismissal we shall have ten days' notice of such intention in advance.

Or we will charter all or any one or two of the above-mentioned boats for $4,000 per month (the condition about notice to apply in this case too)—the Government paying all the expenses of crew, fuel, and provisions—we having the appointment of crews to consist of not less than a captain, a first engineer, a second engineer, a striker, a watchman, a cook, a cabin boy, four firemen, and two deck hands; or we will sell the three boats for $70,000, or either of them for $25,000.

In case of charter being accepted, the boats are not to carry guns for offensive operations.

B.A. SHEPHERD.
F.W. SMITH.
JOHN H. STERRETT.[111]

The Confederate general in charge of the District of Texas, New Mexico and Arizona, Paul Octave Hébert, must have balked at chartering the rebuilt *Bayou City* at $7,500 per month, because a month later, Sterrett submitted another offer, this time for *Bayou City* and her barges for $4,500 per month, with the company absorbing the cost of the crew. Hébert agreed and passed the offer along to his aide-de-camp, who added a notation that the fee would be paid "as soon as the Dept. is provided with funds."[112]

With little else on offer, most of the serviceable riverboats soon found themselves in Confederate service, probably at terms the steamboatmen deemed favorable to the government. (For their part, the government agents likely thought they were getting the short end of the deal, as well.) Soon the boats were running back and forth between Galveston and points around

Steamboats on Buffalo Bayou

Confederate brigadier general Paul Octave Hébert. *Library of Congress.*

Galveston Bay, on Buffalo Bayou and the Trinity River and to landings on the Brazos River by way of the Galveston and Brazos Canal. While the traffic on Buffalo Bayou probably diminished some, thanks to the rail line between Houston and Galveston completed just before the war, the boats and their crews were kept busy with a variety of mundane but necessary tasks, mostly transporting men and supplies around the bay. Sterrett, by far the most experienced and best-known master on the Galveston–Houston run, was appointed superintendent of transports, while simultaneously serving as owner's agent for the charter of *Neptune No. 2*, *Bayou City* and *Mary Hill*.[113] His job of managing the fleet's operations was not too different than the one he'd held with the Houston Navigation Company before the war, although now he was overseeing a much larger collection of boats.

The Texas Marine Department, an organization unique in the Confederacy, combined the roles of a conventional navy, revenue service and military logistics command. The Marine Department operated under the control of the Army, and its boats were kept busy ferrying troops, munitions and supplies between the isolated garrisons around Galveston, taking turns as "guard boats" at the entrance to the bay and, on occasion, exchanging messages and paroled prisoners with the Union blockading force anchored just offshore.[114] The rivermen also appear to have done business with the Confederate authorities on their own accounts; in January 1862 Sterrett provided several hundred barrels of shell (probably oyster shell) to Swiss-born engineer officer Captain Julius Kellersberger for construction of the battery at Fort Point, on the eastern end of Galveston Island, and the following month Curtis Blakeman, the old pilot injured in the *Farmer* explosion some years before, delivered seventy-eight cords of wood to the military garrison at Galveston.[115]

Despite the efforts of the Texas Marine Department and officers like Kellersberger, General Hébert did not believe Galveston could be successfully defended. When Union forces assembled a squadron off the entrance to the harbor and demanded the city's surrender in the fall of 1862, Hébert simply ordered his officers on the scene to stall for time, evacuate the city and spike the guns in the outlying batteries. The senior Confederate officer in Galveston, Colonel Joseph Jarvis Cook, managed to negotiate with the Federals a four-day cease-fire to evacuate non-combatants; during that interval he also managed to remove a large quantity of military stores and some of the artillery pieces that had defended the island. When U.S. Navy Commander William Renshaw's little flotilla of converted ferryboats finally entered the harbor on October 8, they had captured the best harbor in the Confederacy west of Mobile.[116]

For his failure to mount any sort of real defense of the island, Hébert was promptly sacked and replaced by John Bankhead Magruder, a commander from the eastern theater. Magruder had acquired the not-entirely-complimentary nickname of "Prince John" for both his love of amateur theatricals and his elegant sartorial style. Magruder was a capable commander but had run afoul of Robert E. Lee during the Seven Days Battles, when at Malvern Hill (July 1, 1862) a convoluted mix-up of orders resulted in a series of failed assaults against an impregnable Union line. Lee subsequently reorganized his army, and Magruder, having been relieved of command, soon found himself en route to Texas to see what could be made of the mess there.

Magruder's first order of business would be to retake Galveston. Even before he arrived at Houston, he was consulting with Confederate officers who were certain that the island could be recaptured. Chief architect of the plan was military engineer Caleb Forshey, who had taught at a military school in Galveston before the war. Forshey proposed a simultaneous attack by land forces in the town and by gunboats that would engage the Federal fleet in the harbor. Most important, Forshey cautioned Magruder, the attack would have to occur at night, to ensure complete surprise. Forshey's rough outline became the template upon which Magruder's effort to retake the island would be built.[117]

One historian has argued that Magruder's true genius "had always been his ability to pull together seemingly unrelated resources and triumph over a more powerful foe."[118] That would certainly prove to be the case in his attempt to retake Galveston. Magruder immediately set to work cobbling together a makeshift military force from disparate parts—an infantry brigade recently returned from a campaign in New Mexico, artillery pieces from *here*, state militia units from *there*—into a command that might just suffice for the job.

For the naval side of things, though, Magruder had only the Texas Marine Department and its collection of civilian steamboats. These he put under the orders of Leon Smith, a civilian mariner whom he'd known in California years before. Smith, who variously claimed the honorific of captain, major or commodore as the immediate circumstances warranted, had spent much of his life at sea, on steamers running between San Francisco and Panama and with the Morgan Line, which ran boats along the Gulf Coast and Atlantic seaboard.

Magruder selected, probably with Sterrett's guidance, two of the Houston Navigation Company's big passenger packets, *Bayou City* and *Neptune No. 2*, to be the lead boats in the naval assault. On Christmas Day 1862, citing Magruder's authority, Engineer Forshey issued instructions to the local Confederate commander, Colonel DeBray, that the latter officer should

> *summon Capt. Leon Smith, and direct him to prepare the* Bayou City *for service immediately; to put a platform on the boat for the thirty-two pounder rifled cannon, which will be sent to Harrisburg to-morrow; to prepare the* Neptune *in like manner for the two twenty-four-pounder howitzers, now at Harrisburg. He will use cotton on the decks of both to give the appearance of protection, and not wait to fasten it, if it costs time. For this purpose he will use all the mechanics and other force that can be worked with advantage, taking the material and property needed by seizing it, if necessary. He will call for 150 volunteers for each boat, taking citizens and soldiers from all quarters. He will use the small arms already given him. He will be ready to move at noon day after tomorrow to take part in an attack upon the fleet, if things do not change…*[119]

The Galveston–Houston Packet

Leon Smith, commander of the "cottonclad" flotilla at the Battle of Galveston. From Lubbock's *Six Decades in Texas*.

Smith set about converting the boats as best he could, with the materials at hand. *Bayou City* was to carry a single, thirty-two-pounder rifle on her foredeck, while *Neptune No. 2* would be fitted with two twenty-four-pounder howitzers. Scores of cotton bales were stacked, two and three deep, on each boat to a level well above the boiler deck. The cotton, placed "to give the appearance of protection," did provide some security from small arms fire, but that was about all. When a soldier asked Smith what protection the cotton was against artillery, the commodore's answer was blunt: "None whatsoever…our only chance is to get alongside before they hit us."[120] The bales also offered protection to the boilers and machinery on each boat's main deck. The forward end of the superstructure on each boat was closed in with planking, leaving the artillerymen on the foredeck somewhat exposed and vulnerable. From this improvised protection, Smith's boats would be informally known as "cottonclads."

On the hurricane deck of each boat, Smith arranged a pair of boarding devices, one on each side, to mimic the Roman *corvus* from classical times. Probably Smith used the boats' own landing stages, fitted with small anchors or grapnels at the outer end, that could be released to crash down onto an

Steamboats on Buffalo Bayou

Detail view of an eyewitness sketch of the Battle of Galveston, showing the cotton bales stacked "to give the appearance of protection." *Rosenberg Library, Galveston.*

enemy vessel's deck and hold fast. In the heat of battle, men would use the landing stage to rush across to the enemy ship in hopes of capturing her; for now, they loomed high above the makeshift gunboats, poised menacingly against the early winter sky.

The attack was originally planned for the night of December 27, but difficulties in assembling all the forces delayed it until New Year's Eve. Each evening, though, one or more of Leon Smith's boats would creep down the bay, past Red Fish Bar, to probe the Federal fleet's defenses, to see if their appearance was noticed and triggered any response. The Confederates noticed none and became increasingly confident they could pull off a surprise. The Union navy had, in fact, noticed them, and rumors about an imminent Confederate attack had been swirling since Magruder's arrival weeks before.

On the afternoon of the thirty-first, final arrangements were made aboard *Neptune No. 2* and *Bayou City* at Harrisburg. Three hundred dismounted cavalrymen, recently returned from a disastrous campaign in New Mexico, were divided up between the two boats to serve as sharpshooters and, if the opportunity arose, a boarding party. Their commander, Colonel Tom Green, had assembled them before the expedition set out and, with a bit of patriotic hyperbole, called for volunteers for "the most dangerous enterprise that men ever engaged in." So many men stepped forward that officers had to pick and choose among them to narrow them down to the three hundred that could be accommodated. To man the artillery pieces on each boat's foredeck, detachments were counted off from Companies B and C of the First Texas Heavy Artillery. Captain Armand Wier of Company B was in command, supported by Captain E.B.H. Schneider of Company C—the same Captain Schneider who had foolishly marched his company into Buffalo Bayou more than a year and a half before.[121]

The little cottonclad fleet set out from Harrisburg on the afternoon of the thirty-first, with *Neptune No. 2* leading the way, followed by *Bayou City*, the flagship of the expedition, and then *John F. Carr* and *Lucy Gwinn*, which were to be used as tenders to the two bigger boats. Sterrett was in charge of *Lucy Gwinn*. They reached Morgan's Point around sunset and waited there until about 9:00 p.m. While at Morgan's Point, a courier arrived from General Magruder, ordering Smith to bring his little fleet down into the upper part of the Galveston Bay and to wait there until he heard the rumble of Magruder's artillery opening fire on the Federals. Only then, Magruder warned, should Smith commit his flotilla to the action.[122]

Once he got underway, though, Smith may have pushed his instructions well beyond Magruder's intent, as one source describes the cottonclad fleet creeping to within two miles of the harbor at Galveston by one o'clock in the morning. (See Battle of Galveston map, Event 1.) There they hove to and waited. Smith had been told to expect Magruder's bombardment to start at midnight, but so far he had heard nothing. Smith signaled for *Neptune No. 2* to come alongside, and the senior officers held a brief council of war. About this same time, lookouts spotted colored signal lights flashing back and forth between the Federal vessels in the harbor, which Smith correctly took to mean that they had been spotted. Smith ordered the flotilla to fall back up the bay to Half Moon Shoals, about seven statute miles north of Galveston. Here they continued to wait until about 4:00 a.m. when, having heard neither gunfire to indicate the land attack had begun nor had any communication from Magruder, Smith ordered a further withdrawal to Red Fish Bar, where they would be out of sight of the Federals at dawn.[123]

What Leon Smith could not know was that, even as he reluctantly turned his boats north toward Red Fish Bar, General Magruder was pressing forward, still scrambling to get his forces into position. He had carefully assembled his force at Fort Hébert, at the mainland end of the railroad trestle connecting to Galveston, and had arranged to have the trestle planked over with wood

Key events in the Battle of Galveston, as explained in the text. *Map by the author.*

to enable artillery, wagons and hundreds of infantry to pass over easily. The artillery was especially important, as it formed the core of his land force. Between the guns Colonel Cook had managed to remove from Galveston during the cease-fire the previous October and other artillery he had managed to scrape together since, Magruder now had a remarkable twenty-one guns at his disposal—six pieces of siege artillery, fourteen field pieces and a gun mounted on a flat rail car, protected (like his steamers) by bales of cotton. All depended on his artillery and the cottonclads; no amount of infantry, no matter how brave, would be able to strike a blow at the Union ships in the harbor.

But Magruder and his staff had failed to anticipate the stubbornness of the mules in the Confederates' artillery train, who balked at stepping out on the planked-over rail trestle and refused to budge. After a long and futile effort to get them moving across the bridge, the exasperated soldiers removed their harnesses, picked up the traces themselves and started out. Precious time had already been lost, but it soon got worse: Magruder received a report that the Federal fleet in the harbor was signaling, and he assumed that his land force had been detected. Still more than four miles from their assigned positions, the Confederate troops now received orders to follow a circuitous route to the waterfront, in the dark, using back roads and paths few of them were familiar with. It would be three hours more before everyone was in position.

Finally, just after 4:00 a.m.—and four hours late—all was ready. Magruder positioned himself at a field piece along the waterfront at Twentieth Street, aimed at the Union gunboat *Owasco*, lying just opposite in the harbor (Event 2). Magruder jerked the gun's lanyard, setting it off with a roar. The theatrical officer then turned to the gun's crew and reportedly said, "I have done my best as a private; I will go and attend to that of a general."

Soon the firing became general, up and down the waterfront (Event 3). The only Federal troops in the city were a few companies of the Forty-second Massachusetts Infantry, who had billeted themselves on Kuhn's Wharf, near the head of Eighteenth Street. Some of the Confederates' smaller artillery pieces had been hauled onto the upper floors of buildings overlooking the harbor and were now firing both at the beleaguered Massachusetts soldiers and on Federal ships. Colonel Cook took command of the second phase of the attack. The wharf could not be taken by direct assault; the Massachusetts infantry was safe behind hastily built barricades, and near the shoreward end of the wharf, all but a single, narrow plank had been pulled up, making it necessary for anyone approaching the barricade to proceed single file. Cook's troops had prepared for this and carried ladders that, they planned, would allow them to wade out into the gradually deepening harbor and clamber up directly onto the wharf. They plunged ahead in the dark, cold water, braving sporadic (and largely inaccurate) fire from the Federals on the wharf, only to discover that the ladders were either too short or settled into the oozy bottom when the soldiers tried to scale them. Cook's men withdrew, scrambling wet and chilled back onto the shore (Event 4).

By now it was beginning to get light, and the gunners on ships in the harbor were able to accurately target the Confederate batteries on shore (Event 5). Many Union shells also went well wide of their marks, striking buildings and causing casualties across the city. The Confederate attack had lost its momentum, and troops began seeking refuge behind whatever structure looked solid and out of the Federals' line of fire (Event 6). With sunrise approaching, and no news whatever of his cottonclad fleet, Magruder began giving orders for his troops to fall back (Event 7). The attempt to retake Galveston from the Federal occupation appeared to be a complete failure.

Fourteen miles north-northwest of Galveston, at Red Fish Bar, Leon Smith may have heard the report of Magruder's initial shot rumbling across the water. The sound was followed by more guns, until everyone on deck must have heard it clearly. The loud clang of engine-order bells was followed by a churning, thrashing of the water around the steamboats' paddlewheels, and they were off again for Galveston harbor. Firemen bundled resinous pine knots and other hot flammables into the fireboxes to generate more steam.

Even so, it must have taken the cottonclads well over an hour to reach the western end of the harbor. The sky was becoming brighter in the east. As soon as they could clearly make out the nearest Federal warship, which proved to be USS *Harriet Lane*, the Confederate gunners on *Bayou City* opened fire (See Buffalo Bayou and Galveston Bay Map, Event 4). Captain Armand Wier, the artillery officer from the First Texas Heavy Artillery, had already fired off three rounds with the big thirty-two-pound rifle when a bystander, caught up in the adventure of the moment, suggested Wier give the Federals a New Year's present on his behalf. Wier nodded and replied, "Here goes your New Years present!" and yanked the lanyard. The breech of the gun burst, killing Wier instantly and wounding several men of the gun's crew standing nearby. Wier's fellow company commander in the First Texas Heavy Artillery, Captain Schneider, lost an eye to the flying metal. After a period of recovery, Schneider would return to Confederate service as a recruiting officer and live until January 1, 1903—forty years to the day—as a minor hero of the Battle of Galveston, his disastrous attempt at close-order drill on the banks of Buffalo Bayou forgotten by almost all.[124]

Bayou City continued on. The tide was running out, moving along with the boat and making it hard to steer. In her first attempt to strike and board the former revenue cutter, barely under control as she was pulled along by the tide, the cottonclad ran under *Harriet Lane*'s bow, damaging the cottonclad's pilothouse. On *Bayou City*'s upper deck, the soldiers cut the lines on the portside gangway, hoping to latch on to the Union gunboat, but the distance between the vessels was too great, and the boarding stage crashed into the water. The heavy gangway dragged astern, sweeping its guy lines along and further wrecking the boat's pilothouse. *Bayou City* steamed on past the Union gunboat, as the men aboard scrambled to clear away the wreckage and get the boat back under control.[125]

Now *Neptune No. 2*, close behind *Bayou City*, steered for *Harriet Lane*. As the two twenty-four-pounder howitzers on her foredeck opened fire on the Union gunboat, the steamboat's master, William H. Sangster, tried to bring *Neptune No. 2* close up on the Union gunboat's starboard side. *Harriet Lane* had gotten underway, though, and this cottonclad was finding it as hard to steer as her consort had. *Neptune No. 2* slammed hard into *Harriet Lane*'s starboard side, crunching and splitting the cottonclad's bow timbers as she did. *Harriet Lane* continued slowly forward, and Sangster brought *Neptune No. 2* around under the Union gunboat's stern, with Confederate sharpshooters sweeping *Lane*'s deck with rifle fire. Reports reached the pilothouse that the cottonclad was flooding, and Sangster wisely abandoned the attack on the Federal vessel and steered his boat for shallow water. *Neptune No. 2* settled in six or eight feet of water near the St. Cyr Wharf, while sharpshooters on her upper deck continued plinking away at any Union officer or sailor who exposed himself above *Harriet Lane*'s bulwark (Event 8).

Bayou City, meanwhile, headed first toward the wharves and then swung around to the left, coming back again on *Harriet Lane*'s port quarter. At this moment, the Federal gunboat had begun to back her engines, the paddlewheels running astern. The cottonclad struck the Union gunboat squarely this time, just aft of the latter's port paddlewheel. The impact heeled *Lane* over to starboard, and as she rolled back level, the iron frame of her turning paddlewheel punched through the Confederate vessel's deck. About this same time, either the shock of the collision or a lucky shot carried away one of *Lane*'s catheads, the heavy timber used to suspend a ship's anchor out over the water, away from the hull. The anchor splashed into the harbor, killing the Federal warship's way and effectively immobilizing her. The Union vessel was now locked in combat with the Confederate gunboat (Event 9).[126]

Though Colonel Green's men had little experience in maritime combat, storming an enemy position was something they understood very well, and they swarmed across from the cottonclad to the Federal warship. There was a short, sharp fight on deck, and it was quickly over. *Harriet Lane*'s commander, Jonathan M. Wainwright, had been killed by an earlier shot and his executive officer, Edward Lea, mortally wounded. The Stars and Stripes were quickly hauled down. Green's horsemen, many of whom had

Eyewitness sketch of the aftermath of the Battle of Galveston, showing *Harriet Lane* and *Bayou City* locked together at center left and the sunken *Neptune No. 2* at extreme left. *Rosenberg Library, Galveston.*

probably never been aboard a ship twenty-four hours previously, had taken one of the most veteran ships of the Union navy. Green's dismounted cavalry would afterward be known as the Confederacy's "horse marines" for their action this day.

With *Harriet Lane* now in Confederate hands, and the soldiers of the Forty-second Massachusetts hopelessly pinned down on Kuhn's Wharf, the action was all but over. The steamer *Owasco* closed to within 300 yards of the locked, immobile pair of *Harriet Lane* and *Bayou City*, then went about when the Confederates on board the latter ship prominently displayed their Federal prisoners on deck, effectively using them as human shields.

Two miles away, the senior Union naval commander, William Renshaw, had been kept completely out of the action by a stroke of misfortune (Event 10). His ship, the converted New York ferryboat *Westfield*, had gotten underway in the early morning darkness in an effort to close with and identify the steamers that had been reported north of Galveston. Unfortunately, he had no local pilot on board to guide him past the shoals, and his ship grounded hard on Pelican Spit. Running aground would have been a problem regardless, but now the timing was disastrous—it was near high tide, and the falling tide would assure that *Westfield* remained stranded until the next high tide, hours away. And there *Westfield* remained, distant and impotent, through the Confederate attack on Kuhn's Wharf, the bombardment of the waterfront by the other Union gunboats and the capture of *Harriet Lane*.

The firing eventually died away, and in due course, Renshaw's stranded vessel was approached by a boat bearing Richard Law, commander of the

Union gunboat *Clifton*. Law explained that the harbor was under a flag of truce. Henry Lubbock, captain of *Bayou City*, had come aboard Law's ship and demanded the surrender of all the Union vessels in the harbor. Under the terms offered, the Federals would be allowed to keep one vessel, to gather up the crews of the other ships and remove them safely to Union territory. It was an audacious bluff, relying as it did on the threat of the Confederates turning *Harriet Lane*'s guns on her former allies. But Law and Renshaw were unaware of the disabled status of that ship, and the threat seemed real enough. Renshaw angrily refused but also knew he could not now save his own ship. He had the crew transferred to other Union vessels nearby and had turpentine and flammable materials spread all over *Westfield*'s deck. Renshaw himself lit the fuse to the powder train to the ship's magazine. Exactly what happened next is unclear—either the fuse burned too quickly to allow Renshaw and his boat's crew to escape, or he and the men did manage to get off a safe distance but returned to *Westfield* when the magazine didn't detonate as expected. In any case, with a thunderous concussion, *Westfield* exploded, killing Renshaw and his boat's crew instantly

Another eyewitness sketch of the Battle of Galveston, showing the sunken *Neptune No. 2* (upper right), *Harriet Lane* and *Bayou City* (center) and the Union gunboat *Owasco* (left). *Rosenberg Library, Galveston.*

(See Buffalo Bayou and Galveston Bay Map, Event 5). It was about 8:45 a.m. on New Year's Day 1863.

After this last unexpected setback, the remaining Union ships got underway and, still nominally under a flag of truce, steamed out of the harbor. Law, now senior officer of the Union squadron, even failed to have his ships take up blockading positions off the entrance to Galveston Bay and instead took his ships all the way to New Orleans to report the calamity. The Confederates made some small attempt to pursue, but in fact, they had won an almost complete victory, one that had very nearly been lost before the arrival of Leon Smith's little cottonclad flotilla. The Union would not attempt to take Galveston again, and the island city would hold the distinction of being the only Confederate port that, once taken by the Union, would be recaptured by the Confederacy.

Just as the sudden detonation of *Westfield* rattled the crews of the remaining Union ships in Galveston harbor, so too the recapture of Galveston rattled the confidence of Union naval officers on blockade duty in the Gulf of Mexico. Many Federal officers had a bit of "ram fever" during the war,[127] with the havoc wrought by the Confederate casemate ram *Virginia* a few months before being fresh in their minds. *Bayou City* seems to have caused more than a few worried headaches for the officers of the blockading squadron, for the converted packet is listed several times in dispatches to the Navy Department. Federal commodore H.H. Bell, who reestablished the Union blockade off Galveston, was convinced by *Bayou City*'s collision with *Harriet Lane* that the cottonclad was built specifically as a ram. Not long after arriving at Galveston, Bell wrote that "a formidable looking ram, having one smokestack, looking like the *Bayou City*, came down the bay and took station at Pelican Spit." The Union navy's fear of *Bayou City* may have done more to protect Galveston than any number of coastal artillery pieces.[128]

Rear Admiral David Farragut, commanding the Union's West Gulf Blockading Squadron, was both dismayed and infuriated at the Galveston debacle. He had Law court-martialed and suspended from the navy for abandoning the blockade of Galveston and wrote that a tension, a nervousness, a "nightmare" had afflicted his officers. "All our disaster at Galveston has been caused by it," Farragut wrote. The assistant secretary of the navy, Gustavus Fox, wrote to Farragut that "the Galveston disaster is the most melancholy affair ever recorded in the history of our gallant navy. Five naval vessels driven off by a couple of steam scows with one gun which burst at the third fire and the attack made by soldiers, our prestige is shaken."[129]

A year before, Confederate general Paul Hébert had judged Galveston Island to be indefensible. Now, at the beginning of 1863, the officer who had retaken it was determined not to let it change hands again. General Magruder quickly turned the island into an armed camp. The engineering officers who had helped plan the recapture of Galveston were set to work building miles of earthworks and forts, some of which were connected by rail to enable the rapid transfer of guns and munitions. Many hundreds of slaves were contracted from area planters to do most of the actual labor. Piles were driven in lines across the harbor to prevent Union warships from entering unmolested as they had in October 1862, and mines were placed, as well. *Neptune No. 2* was left where she was, sunk in shallow water by the St. Cyr Wharf, and finally had her machinery salvaged in June 1863. *Bayou City*, having proved the concept of the cottonclad, was formally purchased by the state and permanently fitted out as a gunboat soon after the battle. The national Confederate government eventually purchased *Bayou City* from the Texas Military Board for $50,000, "which sum reimburses the State in full for all cost and expenditures on said vessel."[130]

In the fall of 1863, Superintendent Sterrett was requested to provide a status report on the vessels being operated by the Texas Marine Department. His report offers a useful snapshot of the department in late October of that year, providing as it does not only a list of vessels (several of which operated on other streams, including the Trinity, Sabine and Brazos Rivers), but also notes on their location and condition:

> *Steamer* Sunflower *(chartered), now undergoing repairs at Beaumont; will soon be in running order; light draft.*
> *Steamer* Grand Bay *(chartered), in the engineer department; not in good order; some work to be done to her heaters, but can run for a short time; very light draft of water.*
> *Steamer* Uncle Ben *(owned by Government), in good order; now running as a transport, but of heavy draft of water, say 3 feet, light.*
> *Steamer* Roebuck *(chartered), in very bad order; not in a condition to run without undergoing heavy repairs; heavy draft, say 3 feet.*
> *Steamer* Jeff Davis *(chartered), laid up; broken shaft; not of much service.*
> *Steamer* Dime, *tender to gunboats; very small.*

Steamers in Galveston Bay.
Steamer Island City *(owned by Government), now running as a food transport; not in good order, but can be run for a few weeks.*
Steamer Colonel Stell *(owned by Government), now as a transport in the engineer department; in good order; just repaired; light draft.*
Steamer Lone Star *(chartered), in the engineer department, at shipyard; will be ready to run on next Friday; in very good order; just repaired, and very light draft of water.*
Steamer A. S. Ruthven *(chartered) at shipyard; will be ready to run on next Friday; in very good order; just repaired, and very light draft of water.*
Steamer Era No. 3, *on the Brazos River, from Columbia to Velasco; wants repairs; can run a short time; light draft.*
Steamer Lucy Gwin *(owned by Government), in Matagorda Bay; in good order; just repaired; she is under control of Colonel [W.R.] Bradfute; she is of very light draft.*
I would say that the Government owns three barges. Two in good order; engineer department using one, and the transport department using one for transportation of wood. The third barge has to be repaired, lying sunk on the flats at Galveston.[131]

Sterrett's list underscores the difficulty of keeping the Marine Department's boats in operation. Fully half the boats were mechanically deficient by this point, a bit past what would become the midpoint of the war. Phrases like "undergoing heavy repairs" and "not in a condition to run" appear throughout the document. Riverboats like those making up the Texas Marine Department had short life expectancies even in the best of times; a shortage of materials and hard, constant running inevitably took its toll on the boats. Still, they soldiered on, ferrying men, supplies and materiel to posts around the bay and other parts of the coast.

In early August 1864, Admiral Farragut's ships forced the entrance to Mobile Bay, closing off that port as a destination for blockade runners operating from Cuba. Up to this point, Galveston and the rest of Texas had been too far removed from the seat of the war, east of the Mississippi, to be of much interest to the runners. After the Battle of Mobile Bay, though, Galveston was the only substantial port on the Gulf of Mexico remaining in Confederate hands. Every several days, a long, low steamship would run in or out of the port under cover of darkness, in aggregate more than a hundred entrances and departures, mostly in the last few months of the conflict.¹³² These stealthy visitors included some of the most famous blockade runners of the conflict, among them *Will o' the Wisp*, which was wrecked on the Gulf beach south of the city in February 1865, and *Denbigh*, a ship that had caused such frustration to Farragut off Mobile that he described her master as "a bold rascal, and well he may be, for if I get him he will see the rest of his days of the war in the [Federal military prison in the] Tortugas."¹³³

During the resurgence of naval activity around the harbor, the few remaining serviceable transports of the Texas Marine Department continued their work, assisting with the maintenance of harbor defenses, setting out signals for the runners and towing the runners in and out of the harbor. Occasionally, more exciting events arose. One dark night in April 1865, just days after Lee's surrender to Grant at Appomattox, the famous Confederate naval officer John Newland Maffitt (1819–1886) got his runner, *Owl*, aground on Bird Key, a sandbar just off the entrance to the bay. Maffitt managed to signal his predicament to soldiers on shore, and Captain McGarvin took the old Buffalo Bayou steamer *Diana* out to provide assistance. *Diana* and another runner, the British steamer *Lark*, managed to get Maffitt's ship off the sandbar and safely into harbor before dawn.¹³⁴ The Federal blockading squadron off Galveston never knew they were there.

But no amount of bold action like Captain McGarvin's could stave off the inevitable collapse. Weeks later, after a flurry of negotiations, the Federal fleet steamed into Galveston harbor unopposed on June 5, 1865.¹³⁵ Galveston had been the last Confederate port to fall.

Chapter 6

REBUILDING

Under such favorable auspices, there cannot be a doubt that these new steamers will be liberally patronized and well supported by the public.
—The Galveston News, *on the introduction of the new steamers* Silver Cloud *and* St. Clair *to the Buffalo Bayou route.*

Commerce returned with renewed vigor after the war. Though the Confederate bank notes held by many loyal Southerners were now worthless—they had never been worth their face value to begin with—enough people were able to buy that the merchants were able to offer a wide variety of goods that hadn't been seen on store shelves in years. With the Union blockade ended and European and Northern markets opened to Texas cotton once again, the packets stood ready to reclaim their old role as the vital and profitable link between inland Texas and the sea.

But if the men and cargo stood ready to resume the trade, the boats did not. Four years of alternating neglect and overwork had left the few remaining antebellum boats in a sorry condition to resume the trade. Nevertheless, the steamboatmen did the best they could with the vessels at hand. In mid-June 1865, even before Federal troops occupied Galveston and formally ended hostilities, the steamers *Lone Star, A.S. Ruthven,* and *Mary Hill* began making regular runs between Houston and Galveston.[136]

The first new boat to arrive and enter the trade after the war was *Arizona*, which tied up to the Houston wharf on the first day of September 1865.[137] She was followed a few months later by the packets *Silver Cloud* under the command of John Sterrett, and *St. Clair*, Captain Curtis Blakeman, both purchased by Sterrett and outfitted for the Buffalo Bayou trade. The local press offered glowing reports on the new boats, noting Sterrett's "reputation for attention to passengers and for keeping the best table anywhere to be met with…Under such favorable auspices," the *Galveston News* concluded, "there cannot be a doubt that these new steamers will be liberally patronized and well supported by the public."[138]

Left unstated was that both *St. Clair* and *Silver Cloud* had been bought new by the U.S. Navy during the war and put into service as gunboats on the Mississippi. Their main decks were fitted with lightweight metal plating to provide some protection around the boilers and other machinery, but this was really only sufficient to protect against small arms fire. This flimsy armor earned boats like this the derisive nickname of "tinclads"— as opposed to properly armored, ironclad naval vessels—and they were used primarily for patrols along the river, trying to intercept the passage of men and materiel between Confederate-held territory on either side of the Mississippi.

The 203-ton sternwheeler *St. Clair* had been launched at Belle Vernon, Pennsylvania, in 1862 and was intended to run between Pitttsburgh and St. Louis. On her first visit to that latter port, however, she was bought by the Federal government and commissioned as Tinclad No. 19.[139] *St. Clair*

Rare photo of *St. Clair* as a Union "tinclad" gunboat. *Wilson's Creek National Battlefield, National Park Service.*

participated in several small engagements as part of the navy's Mississippi Squadron, including the relief of Fort Donelson in January 1863, convoying supply transports in support of Union forces besieging Vicksburg in the spring and summer of that year, and the Red River campaign in 1864.

Silver Cloud had been launched at Brownsville, Pennsylvania, also in 1862. At 236 tons, *Silver Cloud* was slightly larger than *St. Clair*.[140] *Silver Cloud* saw less combat on the Mississippi than her consort but did carry Union general William Tecumseh Sherman from Memphis to Vicksburg in early 1864.[141] *Silver Cloud*'s most dramatic service came in April 1864 when she came upon the aftermath of the infamous Confederate assault on Fort Pillow, several miles north of Memphis. Confederate troops under the command of Nathan Bedford Forrest had stormed the fort and, finding it manned by African American Union soldiers, had gone on a killing rampage even after the survivors of the assault had abandoned the fort and tried to flee into the river. *Silver Cloud* was met on the bank by some Confederates with a flag of truce, who offered a few hours' cease-fire during which the boat's crew could carry off the wounded and attend to the dead. The boat's commanding officer, William Ferguson, readily agreed. One of his junior officers, Acting Master's Mate Robert S. Critchell, later described what they found:

> We then landed at the fort, and I was sent out with a burial party to bury our dead. I found many of the dead lying close along by the water's edge, where they had evidently sought safety; they could not offer any resistance from the places where they were, in holes and cavities along the banks; most of them had two wounds. I saw several colored soldiers of the Sixth United States Artillery, with their eyes punched out with bayonets; many of them were shot twice and bayoneted also. All those along the bank of the river were colored. The number of the colored near the river was about seventy. Going up into the fort, I saw there bodies partially consumed by fire. Whether burned before or after death I cannot say, anyway, there were several companies of rebels in the fort while these bodies were burning, and they could have pulled them out of the fire had they chosen to do so. One of the wounded negroes [sic] told me that "he hadn't done a thing," and when the rebels drove our men out of the fort, they (our men) threw away their guns and cried out that they surrendered, but they kept on shooting them down until they had shot all but a few. This is what they all say.
>
> I had some conversation with rebel officers and they claim that our men would not surrender and in some few cases they "could not control their men," who seemed determined to shoot down every negro soldier, whether

he surrendered or not. This is a flimsy excuse, for after our colored troops had been driven from the fort, and they were surrounded by the rebels on all sides, it is apparent that they would do what all say they did, throw down their arms and beg for mercy.[142]

Both Sterrett, who commanded *Silver Cloud*, and Blakeman, in *St. Clair*, had run steamboats for the Confederacy during the war, and seem to have kept mum about their new boats' role in the "late unpleasantness," presumably to avoid putting off potential customers. Their reticence on that subject seems to have worked, for the local press appears never to have mentioned their previous incarnation as Union gunboats. A few weeks after their arrival, the *Galveston Weekly News* commented on a series of northers that had caused several boats to become stranded. *Silver Cloud* and *St. Clair* had not, the paper noted, "and the reason doubtless is that they were constructed expressly for our trade."[143]

Sterrett operated his two new boats for several months on his own, under the name of "Sterrett's Galveston and Houston Daily Line of Steamers." By 1866, a half dozen boats were in service running between Houston and Galveston, including *T.M. Bagby, Silver Cloud, St. Clair, Shreveport, Rob Roy* and *Arizona*, and several others were running the same route intermittently. *Silver Cloud* did not survive the year, though, being snagged and sunk in the bayou in October 1866, just above Harrisburg, with no loss of life. (See Buffalo Bayou and Galveston Bay Map, Event 6.)[144]

The war had destroyed the old Houston Navigation Company, but many of the company's old investors remained, and rejoined to create a new company to emulate the success of the old one. They organized the Houston Direct Navigation Company in October 1866, with the chartered directive to operate "a sufficient number of steamers and barges to meet the demands of Commerce." Among its corporate officers were Sterrett, who continued in personal command of company boats, and William Marsh Rice (1816–1900), a successful merchant whose estate would found the prestigious private university in Houston bearing his name. The City of Houston reportedly backed the company with $200,000 in public funds.[145]

To most travelers, the new enterprise was little different than the old one from before the war. It offered daily service between the two cities, and several of the new boats, including *Diana*, bore familiar names. But under Sterrett's stewardship, the new company embarked on two new avenues of business. The most important of these was that the company would begin transferring passengers and cargo to and from seagoing ships—particularly the "little red steamers" of the Morgan Line—in the anchorage off Galveston. (See

Steamboats on Buffalo Bayou

St. Clair at the Houston steamboat landing, circa 1867. At lower right, a new boat has just arrived and is offloading her cargo. *Houston Metropolitan Research Center.*

Buffalo Bayou and Galveston Bay Map, Event 7.)[146] In theory, this would allow the company and its shippers to avoid the high tariffs and warehousing fees imposed by the Galveston Wharf Company.

One passenger who rode the packets up to Houston during this period was Johannes Swenson, a young Swede who, with about one hundred other young people, immigrated to Texas shortly after the Civil War. After a harrowing passage from New York in the summer of 1867, Swenson and his comrades found themselves anchored at quarantine off Galveston. After three days, the port's medical officer lifted the quarantine and permitted the immigrants to proceed to their respective destinations. Swenson boarded a riverboat in the harbor and, without setting foot on Galveston Island, proceeded up the bay toward Houston. Aboard the packet, Swenson later recalled,

> We got the first good meal since we left New York…it was a beautiful moonlit night. How delightful it was to stand on deck and let the leaves of the trees on shore pass between the fingers. About midnight the ship stopped

to take on wood. I shall never forget how glorious it felt to put the feet on solid ground again. It was also the first time on Texas soil. After the wood had been loaded, the ship continued up the bay and at four in the morning we were in Houston.[147]

The idea of transferring goods and passengers directly from one vessel to another was innovative and, for a time, effective. But the island wharves effectively countered the practice by increasing the fees Sterrett's boats had to pay when they landed to wood and load return cargo, giving the packet line little incentive to transfer goods and passengers "direct." In time, the practice died off, and the packets returned to their traditional terminals along the waterfront downtown.[148]

The second new aspect to the Direct Navigation Company's operations was a prescient decision of Sterrett's to purchase a pair of small, powerful

Buffalo Bayou Ship Channel Company Dredge *City of Houston* in Buffalo Bayou, circa 1870. The B.B.S.C.Co. was chartered in 1869 with the expressed purpose of improving the bayou for navigation by seagoing vessels. *Houston Metropolitan Research Center.*

tugs, *Superior* and *Ontario*. These tugs would be used for towing heavy cotton barges to Galveston.[149] Perhaps Sterrett recognized that the revitalized railroads, which could whisk riders between the two cities in under three hours, would gradually bleed off the passenger trade upon which his boats had depended. This early, firm step into the towing business gave the Houston Direct Navigation Company an edge that would allow it to survive the end of the passenger packet era.

It was during this same postwar period that the steamboatmen first began to encounter serious competition from the railroads. Traveling by rail in those days could be a bone-rattling, sooty experience, and many passengers continued to patronize the slower, stately riverboats. While the Direct Navigation Company dominated the water route between Galveston and Houston, from 1865 the Galveston, Houston and Henderson Railroad began gradually to draw away the passenger trade by promising a faster, if somewhat less serene, journey.

The first rail trestle connecting Galveston to the mainland, and thence to Houston, had been completed in 1860, just before the war. But it made little impact at the time because, like the packets first testing the Buffalo Bayou route a quarter century before, creating a functioning rail network was a somewhat haphazard, trial-and-error system. Construction of railroads had begun in earnest in the 1850s, with several different lines extending out from Houston. By the time Texas seceded from the Union in February 1861 and cast its lot with the Confederacy, rail lines had been established west as far as Richmond, on the Brazos River, as far north as Millican (near Navasota), to the Sabine River and the Louisiana border to the east and Galveston to the southeast. But none of these lines connected with any other railroad connected to the rest of the country, and worse, they were all of different gauges, making it impossible for a single locomotive or piece of rolling stock to travel any great distance. Freight and passengers alike were forced to change trains and railroads frequently, which further limited their popularity as a means of conveyance.

Sterrett's Direct Navigation Company made efforts to adapt to the expansion of the railroads, offering freight transfers to the Buffalo Bayou, Brazos and Colorado Railroad at Harrisburg.[150] The company did reasonably well, expanding to operating five passenger boats on the bayou by 1870, *T.M. Bagby, Diana, Charles Fowler, Lizzie* and *J.H. Whitelaw*; a smaller, freight-only sternwheeler, *Henry A. Jones*; and numerous barges, along with the tugs *Superior* and *Ontario*. By the following year, 1871, the aggregate tonnage of vessels, of all owners, operating regularly on Buffalo Bayou was approaching five thousand tons:

Houston Direct Navigation Company freight boat *Lizzie* loading at the Houston landing, circa 1872. *Houston Metropolitan Research Center.*

Vessels Navigating Buffalo Bayou[151]

Name	Class	Length (ft.)	Beam (ft.)	Tonnage Measurement
T.M. Bagby	Steamboat	175	50	508
Diana	do. [ditto]	171	32	450
Henry Jones	do.	130	32	275
Era No. 3	do.	140	32	377
Mary Conley	do.	125	32	300

Steamboats on Buffalo Bayou

Name	Class	Length (ft.)	Beam (ft.)	Tonnage Measurement
S. J. Lee	do.	130	29	200
Caddo	do.			250
C. K. Hall	do.			120
Royal Arch	do.			65
Bagdad	do.			225
Wren	do.			301
Crescent	Tug			140
Buck	do.			10½
Alert	do.			
Superior	do.			14
Ontario	do.			8
Seven (7) Barges	[no data in orig.]	126	26	959
Twenty-one (21) small schooners	[no data in orig.]			602
Total tonnage:				**4,804½**

The Galveston–Houston Packet

In the summer of 1870 Sterrett brought a new boat into the Buffalo Bayou trade, *Diana*. She was a big boat at 452 tons, though was described as being a bit smaller than her Direct Navigation Company stablemates *J.H. Whitelaw* (actually smaller at 439 tons) and *T.M. Bagby* (508 tons).[152] Sterrett brought her direct from the builder's yard at Cincinnati, where he supervised the fitting of her engines and took on a load of furniture bound for Galveston. The new boat, the *Galveston Daily News* informed its readers, had cabins "free from the tinsel and gaudy ornamentation so popular a year or two since, but have all the accessories necessary to secure the comfort and convenience of passengers." The editor went on to note that, including barges, *Diana* was the thirty-first vessel brought into the bayou trade by Sterrett.[153]

Despite the comforts offered aboard the boats, however, the railroads continued gradually to draw away the passenger trade. Prices for cabin passage lagged, and freight assumed a more prominent place in the advertisements placed in local papers. The freight business seemed strong enough, with the Direct Navigation Company hauling almost two million bales of cotton from Houston to the wharves at Galveston in the twelve years beginning in 1869.[154] But even by the early 1870s, the railroads, particularly the Galveston, Houston and Henderson that ran directly from Houston to the island, were siphoning off increasingly large amounts of the trade, even in cotton. While the five years following the Civil War saw a dramatic rebuilding of the Galveston–Houston packet trade to something approaching its prewar prominence, it would be the changes in the next decade that would profoundly change the business and ultimately end the era of steamboating on Buffalo Bayou.

By 1873, the company was running two boats—*Diana*, commanded by Sterrett himself, and *T.M. Bagby*—as passenger packets but also operated three vessels as "freight boats": *Charles Fowler*, *Lizzie* and, under charter, *Henry A. Jones*. The freight boats were advertised "with barges, daily." In addition, the company operated twenty-two barges and three tugs.[155] Nevertheless, by this time, a single railroad, the Galveston, Houston and Henderson, was taking close to double the volume of cotton brought down by *all* the steamboats and barges running on the bayou. The implications of this must have been clear to all concerned; the railroads were not a passing fancy, and the trade they were taking away from the boats was not going to be won back by lower fares and better food in the main salon. The Buffalo Bayou packet trade had already been relegated to second-best, and if it were going to survive in any form, it would have to be transformed. In the coming decade, it would indeed be transformed by consolidation and corporate maneuvering in a way that would allow it to carry on a while longer, but in a form that bore little resemblance to its antebellum dominance.

Chapter 7

MORGAN MOVES IN

I have but little confidence in the project of Mr. Morgan, since looking at his ditch.
—Editor of the Mexia, Texas Ledger, badly misjudging the import of Charles Morgan's new ship channel on Buffalo Bayou.

By 1873, the Direct Navigation Company was a large-scale operation, completely eclipsing a handful of small operators who had been running individual boats on the bayou irregularly, occasionally shifting their operations to the Trinity River or Brazos as business warranted.

Facing increasing competition from the railroads, though, fewer passengers were traveling between Houston and Galveston by way of the bayou. Though more people than ever were moving between the two cities, steamboat fares remained flat, virtually unchanged from the days before the war. In 1868, soon after the Direct Navigation Company was founded, the fare for cabin passage between Houston and Galveston had been three dollars, "supper and berth included." Eight years later, the price was still three dollars. For those willing to bring their own food and seek out a soft bit of planking on the main deck to sleep on, deck passage could be had for as little as one dollar. In 1875, the Houston Direct Navigation Company was running only two dedicated passenger boats, *Charles Fowler* and *Diana*, each making three round trips each week.[156]

The rapid expansion of railroads fanning out from Houston did provide the company with some benefit, boosting the Direct Navigation Company's freight revenues in the early 1870s by carrying iron rails, shipped from foundries and mills in the eastern United States, for use in the construction of

The Galveston–Houston Packet

Houston Direct Navigation Company packet *Diana* at the Galveston wharf, circa 1872. *DeGolyer Library, Southern Methodist University.*

A locomotive of the Galveston, Houston and Henderson Railroad moves cotton cars at Galveston, circa 1870. *DeGolyer Library, Southern Methodist University.*

both the Houston and Texas Central and International and Great Northern Railroads. In 1877, Charles Morgan acquired controlling interest in both the Houston and Texas Central and the Great Northern Railroads, which gave him easy rail access not only across the central part of the state but also north all the way to Denison, Texas, on the edge of the Indian Territory (now Oklahoma), where it connected to the Missouri, Kansas and Texas line, thence to St. Louis, Chicago and beyond.[157]

But generally, the business outlook for freight traffic on Buffalo Bayou remained slow. While the expansion of the railroads across eastern Texas brought increasingly large volumes of cotton into Houston, and thence to the wharves at Galveston, the amounts carried by the boats of the Direct Navigation Company and other operators remained relatively flat during the middle part of the 1870s, varying between about 120,000 and 180,000 bales annually. During that same period, the Galveston, Houston and Henderson Railroad, the single line running between Houston and Galveston, was hauling close to double the volume of cotton brought down by *all* the steamboats and barges running on the bayou:

Sources of Cotton Receipts at Galveston, 1872–77[158]

Received from	**1872–73**	**1873–74**	**1874–75**	**1875–76**	**1876–77**
Other Ports	0	no data	5,967	4,022	3,252
Galveston, Houston & Henderson RR	238,367	**no data**	194,938	266,125	278,746
Gulf, Colorado & Santa Fe RR	0	no data	0	0	28
Buffalo Bayou	118,115	no data	147,417	179,183	130,278
Trinity River	1,732	no data	4,023	5,555	2,034

Brazos River	686	no data	1,697	2,152	753
West Coast	8,804	no data	847	1,096	743
East coast	3,921	no data	5,892	11,194	4,686
Bay Shore	76	no data	113	224	247
Clinton	0	no data	0	0	74,465
Totals	**371,741**		**360,894**	**469,731**	**495,237**

Basic company operations remained much as they had before the war, with the addition of barges, either loaded with cotton or, in some cases, cordwood, to allow the boat to complete the round trip from Houston to Galveston and return without having to refuel at the island. The boats continued to run at night, allowing passengers the full day on either end to conduct business or make travel connections.

Serious accidents involving the packets occurred less frequently in the years after the Civil War, but they were still a cause for concern among the traveling public. A particularly gruesome accident claimed *Henry A. Jones*, under the command of Curtis Blakeman, in early 1873. She left the landing at Commerce Street in Houston at dusk on the evening of February 13 and headed down Buffalo Bayou, carrying 412 bales of cotton and a barge lashed alongside, loaded with cordwood.

It was a dark, moonless night. The first part of the trip passed without incident. But about 5:00 a.m. on Valentine's Day, a couple of miles above Red Fish Bar, those awake heard a loud report, followed almost immediately by shouts of "Fire! Fire!" It appears that the firewall in the boiler casing gave way, sending out from the firebox flames that ignited the loose, ragged bales of cotton stacked nearby. W. Dugat Williams, the first pilot, was on the hurricane deck at the time and, upon hearing the alarm, ran down to the main deck. Seeing that the fire was already too far gone to be stopped, he called to the man at the wheel, assistant pilot Dave S. Gordon, to abandon his post and save himself. Williams, Gordon and some other men made it to the wood barge and cast off from the flaming steamer.

Fifteen miles to the north, the Direct Navigation Company boat *Charles Fowler* had just rounded Morgan's Point and begun the long run down the bay.

Unidentified riverboat captain, Jefferson, Texas, circa 1875. *DeGolyer Library, Southern Methodist University.*

Set against the predawn darkness, the bright orange gleam on the horizon caught the eye of Captain S.P. Christian, who crowded on the steam in a race to the scene. He covered the distance in an hour and twenty-seven minutes. By then, though, *Henry A. Jones* had burned to the waterline. The crew of *Charles Fowler* pulled the chilled survivors from the water and headed for Galveston. (See Buffalo Bayou and Galveston Bay Map, Event 8.) The keeper of the Red Fish Bar lighthouse, two miles from the scene, had also seen the fire and managed to pull two more men from the water with his skiff. Twenty-nine crewmen were saved, including Captains Blakeman, Williams and Gordon. Twenty-three others died. Liability for the boat and its cargo, roughly estimated at $50,000, fell squarely upon the shoulders of the Houston Direct Navigation Company, which had adopted the risky policy of underwriting its own boats.[159]

It was about this same time that the Direct Navigation Company began to benefit more directly from an alliance formed a few years before with Charles Morgan's companies. Morgan had, early on, pioneered the integration of multiple, interconnected modes of transportation, buying up interest in railroads, stagecoach lines and local companies, all of which fed passengers and cargo into his flagship enterprise, the Southern Steamship Company. This allowed the company to operate more efficiently, reduce redundancies and schedule connections between modes of transport much more efficiently. Such arrangements also offered much greater convenience for shippers and the traveling public, by making the entire process of traveling or shipping more convenient. As one example of this streamlining process, in 1873 a person could purchase a single ticket via Morgan Line interests to carry them from San Antonio, 140 miles from the Gulf of Mexico, all the way to New Orleans. The route was complex enough—stagecoach from San Antonio to Cuero, by rail from Cuero to the port of Indianola, on Matagorda Bay, by steamer from Indianola to Galveston, by another steamer from Galveston to Morgan City, Louisiana and thence by rail to New Orleans—but each leg connected with the next, and the full trip was secured by a single ticket purchased through the local agent for the line. In that same period, passengers in Galveston could contact the Morgan Line's local agent, Captain Charles Fowler, and purchase through tickets to destinations as distant as New York, Chicago, St. Louis "and all points north and west."[160]

There was another benefit to the alliance between the Direct Navigation Company and the Morgan Line. As noted earlier, one of the key operational features of the Direct Navigation Company that set it apart from other, prewar lines was that it began transferring passengers and cargo "direct" with other vessels in the harbor at Galveston, without landing there at the wharf. This was done to avoid the Galveston Wharf Company's fees, which were seen as monopolistically high.

Morgan himself knew something about the benefits of holding a monopoly, as he had virtually shut out most of his coastwise shipping competition in the Gulf of Mexico by the time of the Civil War.[161] The Morgan Line's operations were disrupted by the war—many of the company's vessels in Southern ports were seized by Confederate authorities and lost to the

Steamboats on Buffalo Bayou

An unidentified sternwheel steamboat (background) at the Galveston wharf, circa 1875. *DeGolyer Library, Southern Methodist University.*

company forever—but after the conflict, the company returned to the Gulf, as determined to restore Morgan's fortunes there as Sterrett and the investors in the Direct Navigation Company had been on Buffalo Bayou.

In keeping with his determination to control all segments of the transportation network, Morgan found a willing ally in the Houston Direct Navigation Company. In parallel with that organization's incorporation in 1866, a second company had been created, the Texas Transportation Company, with the intent of dredging Buffalo Bayou to a depth that would accommodate deeper draft, seagoing vessels. Little came of this plan, though, and after several years, Morgan formed his own enterprise, the Ship Channel Company, to pursue a similar effort.[162] In 1873, Morgan appealed to the Galveston Wharf Company for a reduction of rates. Morgan was in a strong position now to insist on lower rates for landing cargo from his ships destined for the interior of the state. If the Wharf Company declined, Morgan argued, he would bring his own dredges to Galveston Bay and cut a ten-foot channel all the way to Houston. The day that channel was completed, he warned, would be the last day that one of his steamers landed at the wharves on the island. It was rumored that the directors of the Galveston Wharf Company laughed out loud at that suggestion, to Morgan's face.[163]

Faced with this refusal, Morgan moved to make good on his threat. He bought out the City of Houston's share of the Direct Navigation Company, which made Morgan the largest single shareholder of that enterprise. After delays in 1874 caused by the lingering effects of an international financial panic the year before, Morgan set about his channel project in earnest. He collected boats and dredges at Morgan City, Louisiana, and had them brought over to Galveston Bay. His engineers laid out a route with cuts through Half Moon Shoal and Red Fish Bar. Most important, his dredges began cutting a straight channel directly through the narrow peninsula at Morgan's point, shortening the meandering route through San Jacinto Bay. The draft of seagoing steamships would force them to use the deeper cut through Morgan's Point, effectively giving Charles Morgan absolute control over deep-hulled vessels' access to Buffalo Bayou.

By mid-1875, Morgan had eight dredges, six tugs and twelve movable derricks and barges working on the project, now set to cut a 9-foot-deep, 120-foot wide channel from Galveston Bay to a spot on the north bank of Buffalo Bayou. Here Morgan established a little settlement called Clinton, named after the town in Connecticut where Morgan had been born in 1795. The site was near present-day Galena Park, eleven or twelve miles below the Houston landing, following the meandering course of the bayou. Morgan determined to make Clinton the terminus of his shipping line and began constructing wharves, warehouses and eight miles of railroad to connect them all to Houston and the railroad terminals there.[164] When the first large Morgan steamer tied up at Clinton in September 1876, direct from New York with sixty rail car loads of goods destined for points in the interior of the state scattered along the various railroads fanning out from Houston, that city's *Daily Telegraph* could barely contain its glee at breaking the hold of the Galveston Wharf Company, writing, "This is a practical result beyond quibble and doubt of the Success of the Ship Channel, and proves its reality to the understanding of all. The merchants who received this freight get it free of the extortions of Galveston *bete noir* [sic], its hideous Wharf Monopoly."[165]

Of course, Morgan was just as determined to exploit his new monopoly of deep-water access to Buffalo Bayou as the Galveston Wharf Company had been to take advantage of theirs. The Morgan Line promptly put a chain across its deep-water cut through Morgan's Point, allowing access only to its own vessels and those of affiliated companies. Smaller craft could still follow the meandering, shallower route through San Jacinto Bay or pay a substantial fee. Soon after the channel was completed, the owners of the schooner *George Sealy* were compelled to pay $105.26 to make one round trip through the half-mile-long cut across Morgan's Point, above and beyond the fee for towing the boat up the bayou.[166] The chain across the canal quickly became a none-too-subtle symbol of Morgan's own tight control over waterborne commerce coming in and out of the bayou.

The *Galveston Daily News* was surprisingly dismissive in assessing the impact of the new channel, citing the judgment of the editor of another newspaper who had recently traveled the route. "I can see no injurious effect it will have either on the commerce of Galveston or Houston," he wrote. "I have but little confidence in the project of Mr. Morgan, since looking at his ditch, seeing how the wind can blow the water out of the bay in so short a time." Galveston readers were separately reminded that the Houston Direct Navigation Company would continue to operate in the bayou trade, notwithstanding the traffic of Morgan's ships. No mention was made of the fact that Morgan was, by this time, a major shareholder in the Direct Navigation Company.[167]

The Houston Direct Navigation Company's increasingly close alliance with the Morgan Line would ultimately mean significant changes in the way it did business and a steady shift away from the traditional packet trade that had held sway for nearly forty years. The Morgan Line acquired controlling interest in the Houston Direct Navigation Company in 1877–78. John Sterrett, though, was not around to witness the takeover. In the fall of 1875, with Morgan's work on the channel to Clinton well underway, Sterrett retired from day-to-day involvement in the company. The reason is not clear. While Morgan was not yet majority owner in the company, he was the largest single shareholder and may have worked to push Sterrett aside. For his part, Sterrett may have been unhappy with the company's increasing focus on freight service, and withdrew from the company on his own volition. Or it may simply be that, after almost forty years in the pilothouse, Sterrett was tired. Whatever the reason, Sterrett stepped down, and the company named a steam tug in his honor.[168]

Sterrett certainly would have had plenty to occupy his time away from the boats. John and Susan Sterrett had at least eight children, beginning with a daughter, Henrietta, in 1847. Several girls followed—Josephine, Julia and Ida—and then two boys, William and Warner. Finally, in about 1864, came twins E. Howard and Adelle. Snapshots of the family provided at ten-year intervals by the census suggest that the two older boys might not have survived into adulthood, but by the time he retired from the Direct Navigation Company, John and Susan probably still had several children at home, including the eleven-year-old twins.[169]

The Galveston–Houston Packet

Perhaps looking to start a new venture, in December 1875 Sterrett left for Austin, a city he had seemingly had little involvement with to that point, to take up the proprietorship of the Raymond House hotel. The *Galveston Daily News* noted his departure, suggesting that he would show his guests in Austin the same sort of attention to service and comfort that he had aboard his boats. "That his reputation in this respect will be fully maintained is made evident from the fact that he takes with him from here a full corps of cooks, stewards and waiters. He has made arrangements for receiving regular supplies of fish, oysters, etc from Galveston, and will make all the markets within reach of the State Capital tributary to the cuisine of the Raymond House."[170] Sterrett's tenure there, however, didn't last, because by the following spring the Raymond House had a new proprietor, and Sterrett had presumably returned to Houston.[171]

Sterrett went "over the river" while visiting Galveston on June 18, 1879, at the age of sixty-four. He had, according to his obituary, "amassed more than a competence by the exercise of his head and hands," but "like the majority of old Texans, in his liberal generosity, did not retain much of it, and died a relatively poor man." Though he was gruff and abrupt in his manner, another obituary noted, "no man had a kinder or warmer heart."[172]

John Sterrett hadn't brought the first steamboat to Buffalo Bayou, and he obviously wouldn't command the last boat to tie up at the Main Street landing. But Sterrett had come to Texas, with his little boat *Rufus Putnam*, at a time when the successful arrival of a new boat on the upper reaches of the bayou was a notable thing. Sterrett had helped create the regular steam packet trade between Galveston and Houston and personally superintended the two companies that came to dominate the trade both before and after the Civil War. He supervised the construction and purchase of many of the boats himself. The packet trade, as it reached its zenith in the years immediately after the war, was as much a creation of John Sterrett as of any individual. And yet, in his later years, Sterrett had begun to prepare for the ultimate transformation of that trade into something fundamentally different, with the purchase of steam tugs and a whole fleet of barges in late 1860s and early 1870s. He witnessed, too, the establishment of a deep-water channel that would carry seagoing ships across Galveston Bay and miles up Buffalo Bayou, as well as an alliance with the Morgan Line. The ultimate outcome of all these trends would occur in the decades after Sterrett's death, but it is easy to imagine that the old steamboatman could already see the waning of the era he'd done so much to create and maintain.

Chapter 8

THE FINAL YEARS

> *Down it comes, that old rusty chain stretched across Buffalo Bayou!*
> —*The Houston Daily Post, on the removal of the chain placed by the Morgan Line to block access to Buffalo Bayou to all but its own deep-draft steamships, May 1892.*

Charles Morgan, the New Yorker who had done so much to expand and consolidate transportation networks across the South and the Gulf of Mexico, died in May 1878. His son-in-law and successor, Charles A. Whitney, continued many of Morgan's policies, including maintaining a focus on shutting Galveston out of the trade between the interior of Texas, through Houston and on to the rest of the country. This corporate imperative would steadily and profoundly shape the future of both the Houston Direct Navigation Company and of navigation on Buffalo Bayou itself.

In 1866, as superintendent of the newly formed Houston Direct Navigation Company, John Sterrett had invested heavily in a series of unpowered barges, along with two propeller-driven steam tugs, *Superior* and *Ontario*. The tugs themselves were tiny, at fourteen and eight registered tons, respectively, and were probably used initially in helping to shift the barges around on the bayou.[173] The barges, on the other hand, had hulls almost as large as a medium-sized packet—126 feet long, 26 feet across and nearly 140 registered tons each.[174] Unlike modern barges with their slab-like, steel hulls and sharp angles, Sterrett's barges were finely shaped examples of the shipwright's craft, with a clean "entrance" at the bow and "exit" at the stern, to cut through the water more efficiently. On the foredeck of each barge were placed heavy towing bitts, a capstan and ground tackle, including one or two large anchors. Well aft, above the sternpost, was built a large platform, standing five or six feet proud of the deck to allow anyone standing on to see clearly over the cargo. In the center of the platform stood an enormous steering wheel, six feet or more in diameter, to control the rudder at the stern of the barge. When towed behind another vessel, a helmsman positioned there could maneuver the barge somewhat independently of the tow, not unlike the way an old-fashioned hook-and-ladder fire truck had its own steering mechanism at the rear. Having a towed barge with its own steering capability eased the stress on the towline and greatly reduced the likelihood of collision or accident. Arching over the length of each barge was a single hog chain, running across a series of braces. Like the steamboats themselves, the barges were very lightly built and needed this additional support to maintain the hull's rigidity. Some of the company's barges were simply numbered, but others were named in their own right.[175]

The Houston Direct Navigation Company had announced in May 1877 it would abandon the passenger trade between Houston and Galveston. The

Houston Direct Navigation Company cotton barge at the Bayou City Cotton Compress on Buffalo Bayou, circa 1905. *DeGolyer Library, Southern Methodist University.*

big passenger boats like *T.M. Bagby* and *Diana* were retired. *Bagby* was sold to parties in Mobile, Alabama, and was ultimately dismantled at Dog Island off Mobile Bay. *Diana*, the smaller of the two but generally recognized as the grander of the pair, suffered a less dignified fate: her boilers and machinery were removed, her superstructure cut away above the main deck and she was reconfigured as a barge, in which role she continued to operate until at least 1883.[176]

But freight had always been the big driver of profit, and in that regard, the company continued to keep busy. On occasion, the company was hauling cotton down the bayou to Galveston faster than it could be unloaded there:

> *Early yesterday morning Central wharf was crowded with cotton brought down by the barges of the Houston Direct Navigation Company. Hundreds of men and drays made things lively in that section, removing the valuable consignments to more secure quarters in the press yards. Before they had cleared the wharf, however, the steamer* Lizzie *came in with four heavily laden barges in tow, and, for the want of accommodation, it may be a day or two before they are all unloaded.*[177]

In 1880, the secretary of the Houston Cotton Exchange estimated that the Houston Direct Navigation Company transported 151,349 bales to Galveston and over a quarter million in 1881. Overall, the secretary calculated, the company had transported a fairly staggering mass of freight:[178]

Freight Type	**1880**	**1881**
Cotton	37,837 tons	63,377 tons
Lumber	30,000 tons	55,000 tons
Coal	10,000 tons	15,000 tons
Iron Rails	60,000 tons	30,000 tons
Miscellaneous	41,000 tons	24,500 tons
Totals:	**178,837 tons**	**187,877 tons**

The Galveston–Houston Packet

As previously noted, even in the mid-1870s, the railroads were taking the lion's share of the freight traffic between Galveston and Houston. The large receipts collected by the Houston Direct Navigation Company in the early 1880s likely didn't reflect a change in that pattern, a shift in market share to the steamboats, but rather an overall expansion of trade and commerce in Texas during the postwar period. They were boom years, fueled by inexpensive land and the rapid extension of railroads across the state. In the decade between 1860 and 1870—death and displacement during the Civil War notwithstanding—Texas' population increased by more than 35 percent. It almost doubled again in the decade of the 1870s, and by 1890 the state's population was well over two million persons, an almost four-fold increase in just thirty years.

During this period, the busiest vessel in the Houston Direct Navigation Company's fleet was probably the tug *Louise*, which, during the cotton shipping season in the fall and winter, often made several trips from Houston to Galveston each week. At the beginning of December 1883, for example, *Louise* brought in a string of four barges, loaded with an aggregate haul of 2,215 bales. The *Galveston Daily News* noted that during the previous month, *Louise* had hauled 41,292 bales, and the month before that, 39,085 bales. The previous afternoon, the paper noted, there had been five of the company's barges anchored in the harbor and three more alongside the wharves, "all laden with cotton."[179]

The heavy freight numbers also reflected an improvement in the facilities and handling procedures used by the company. At the urging of the Houston Cotton Exchange, several cotton compresses and new warehouse facilities were set up near Morgan's Clinton facility. "Pressing" the bales, a process that used heavy, steam-powered machinery to compress and tightly bind the bales to allow a maximum number of them to be loaded into a seagoing ship's hold, had long been a process that was undertaken at Galveston, prior to the cotton being loaded onto blue-water vessels for shipment overseas. By encouraging the construction of cotton presses at Clinton, the Houston exchange and the Houston Direct Navigation Company furthered Morgan's goal of shutting Galveston out of the trade as completely as possible. A total of five large compresses were in operation around Clinton by the early 1880s, all sited with rail access on one side and Buffalo Bayou on the other, streamlining the transition from rail car to press to cotton barge to seagoing steamship.[180]

But the wharves at Clinton had never been more than a temporary proposition for the Morgan Line, a stopgap to bypass Galveston until a reliable rail connection could be established between Houston and New

Steamboats on Buffalo Bayou

Galveston harbor as viewed from the deck of a schooner, circa 1885. At center in the distance is one of the few remaining sidewheel steamers running on Galveston Bay. *DeGolyer Library, Southern Methodist University.*

Orleans. The channel to Clinton, furthermore, was never deep enough to accommodate the largest of the line's steamers, making it impractical for vessels steaming directly to and from East Coast ports.[181] For their part, Houstonians over time had become increasingly disenchanted with the Morgan Line's arrangement. Although they welcomed the completion of the new channel on the bayou as far as Clinton, as it broke the bottleneck that Galveston had on traffic to and from Houston and the interior, they also saw the channel as incomplete, expecting that it would eventually bring seagoing steamships all the way to the Main Street landing.[182]

The Morgan Line had been working toward completion of the New Orleans–Houston rail line for several years, contracting with short, existing lines and laying new rails where needed, until the complete route formally opened in the fall of 1880. The line remained only partially operational for many months, though, for lack of a suitable bridge over the Atchafalaya River at Morgan City, Louisiana, and other maintenance issues.[183] These difficulties delayed the Morgan Line's phase-out of the wharves at Clinton,

The Galveston–Houston Packet

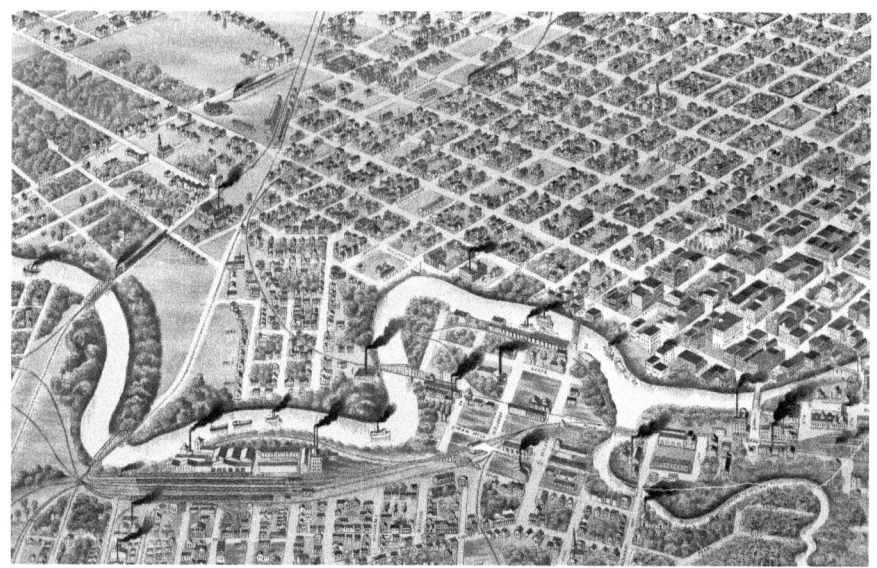

Bird's eye view of Houston, 1891, looking south. The old steamboat landing downtown is at center right, while Buffalo Bayou winds its way toward Galveston Bay, off to the left. Tugs and cotton barges like those used by the Houston Direct Navigation Company dot the bayou. *Library of Congress.*

but through the 1880s, it gradually shifted more and more of its resources to rail transport and, by the summer of 1883, ended its regular steamship service between Louisiana and Clinton on Buffalo Bayou, preferring instead to land at Galveston and send passengers and cargo on by rail, on lines also owned or controlled by the ever-expanding transportation conglomerate.

But even if Morgan's wharves at Clinton did not serve their intended purpose for more than a few years, they were nonetheless profoundly important in the development of Houston's future as a seaport. As noted, Morgan's Ship Channel raised expectations among Houston merchants that such a route might be cut all the way to Houston itself. That had always been a popular subject of discussion, but Morgan's channel had proved the concept. From the time in the mid-1870s when Morgan began digging his channel in earnest, an increasing number of people began looking at it not as a novel solution to get around a specific problem—in this case, the usurious rates demanded by the Galveston Wharf Company—but as a practical template for future commerce on the bayou.

Beginning in the 1870s, the federal government had begun seriously exploring the notion of a deep-water channel up Galveston Bay and Buffalo

Bayou. Even as Morgan's dredges worked to cut his own, proprietary channel, Congress began appropriating annual funds for dredging at Clopper's Bar, Half Moon Shoal and Red Fish Bar. These were seen as an adjunct to improving trade between Galveston, which the Army's Corps of Engineers had designated as a primary port for the American West in 1880. Work soon began on means to improve the depth of water over the bar at the entrance to Galveston Bay, as well.[184]

Morgan's chain across the channel remained in place through the 1880s, effectively giving Morgan interests, including the Houston Direct Navigation Company, exclusive access to the channel for deep-draft vessels. In the meantime, army engineers moved forward with efforts to increase the depth at the entrance to Galveston Bay and the harbor on the island. Charles Morgan's heir, Charles Whitney, died in the fall of 1882 and with him went the nature of the transportation conglomerate as a family enterprise. Within a year, much of the Morgan system was being sold off to a syndicate headed by Collis P. Huntington (1821–1900), one of the "Big Four" (with Leland Stanford, Mark Hopkins and Charles Crocker) that had built the western half of the Transcontinental Railroad in 1865–69. With the assimilation of Morgan's assets in Texas, including the Houston Direct Navigation Company and the Houston and Texas Central Railroad, under the umbrella of Huntington's Southern Pacific Line, the Buffalo Bayou route became part of an interlocking transportation network that stretched from New Orleans across the Southwest to California. By 1885, the transfer of Morgan Line assets to Huntington's Southern Pacific was complete, and the Morgan Line effectively ceased to exist as a corporate entity.

The Houston Direct Navigation Company and the Houston and Texas Central, however, would continue to operate under their own names for years to come.[185] The Direct Navigation Company continued to do a strong volume of business; from 1890 to 1897, the company's barges hauled 2,323,358 bales of cotton down the bayou, averaging around 290,000 bales annually. For three years during that period, 1894 to 1896, the total tonnage hauled by the company was estimated at 386,481 tons, made up of cotton, cotton seed products, grains, wool, molasses, coal, iron, brick and even some livestock.[186]

By 1890, as well, the Corps of Engineers had completed its own channel work on Galveston Bay and was authorized to make an assessment of the value of the cut through Morgan's Point, along with the other improvements made by the Morgan Line over the previous fifteen years. In May 1892, a deal was finally struck, and the corporate remnants of Morgan's old company, now operating as part of the Southern Pacific, received a payment of $92,316.85. Morgan's chain, which had engendered as much or more resentment in the preceding fifteen years as the avaricious rates of the Galveston Wharf Company had in the decade before that, was cut through to the accompaniment of thundering cannon. "Down it comes," the *Houston Daily Post* trumpeted, "that old rusty chain stretched across Buffalo Bayou."[187] Access to the bayou for shipping would now be open to all.

The Houston Direct Navigation Company carried on through the 1890s and into the twentieth century much as it had in the decade before. In September 1900, a hurricane struck Galveston, sweeping the Gulf of Mexico over the island and low-lying coastal areas. An estimated six thousand persons died on the island and another two thousand on the mainland, in what to this day ranks as the deadliest natural disaster in U.S. history. Shipping caught in the harbor was devastated; the Direct Navigation Company had fourteen barges at Galveston at the time, and all but three were wrecked. The three undamaged barges were pressed into service to carry hundreds of the dead out to sea, where the bodies were cast overboard. The little tug *Louise*, which had hauled hundreds of thousands of bales of cotton down to Galveston over the years, went down in the bay near the lighthouse on Red Fish Bar, with two of her crew; "only the top of her smokestack is visible now." Soon after the storm, another of the company's tugs, *Juno*, brought down two barges from the wharf at Clinton, loaded with relief supplies—including four rail cars' worth of "disinfectants"—sent via special train by the *New York World*.[188]

The Direct Navigation Company—it dropped the name "Houston" sometime after the turn of the century—soldiered on for years after as a purely towing operation. In 1913, the company launched a fleet of steel-hulled barges, among the first in the region, with a capacity of at least 1,800 bales each, more than three times that of the old, wooden-hulled craft they replaced.[189] Nonetheless, there is evidence that the company was not faring well, and the new craft sat idle much of the time.

In 1915, another massive hurricane passed over Galveston. The city-wide fire alarm system was one of many basic parts of the city's infrastructure put out of action and, as a result, several fires that broke out in the aftermath of the storm got out of control. One of these destroyed the Galveston offices of the Direct Navigation Company, near the intersection of Twentieth and Post Office Streets. The storm also wrecked the relatively new railroad causeway connecting Galveston Island to the mainland, cutting off rail access for a time. The *San Antonio Light* reported that Direct Navigation Company barges were being pressed into service to bring freight to the island but noted that "due to the fact that freight rates by water and rail from Houston to

Steamboats on Buffalo Bayou

Galveston harbor, 2012. *Author's photo.*

Galveston are the same, the barges had not been used for a considerable length of time until the rail service was interrupted by the storm." Early the following year, in a hearing before the Interstate Commerce Commission in New York looking into allegations that the Southern Pacific had been giving secret rebates to preferred customers, there was testimony that the Direct Navigation Company had only handled cotton in recent years, with all other freight going by rail, and one witness "intimated that [the company] was being operated at a loss." Not long after, the Direct Navigation Company ceased operations. By the fall of 1920, the company's old site at Clinton had been leased to Gray Engineering Works of Galveston, which planned to use the facility for the construction and repair of wooden and steel vessels, barges, tugs, tankers and other craft. The Direct Navigation Company did not disappear from the bayou in a sudden or dramatic way but instead faded gradually, bit by bit, until one day, fifty-odd years after its founding, it simply wasn't there anymore.[190]

After the "old rusty chain" across the Morgan Line's private ship channel came down in 1892 and maintenance of the waterway became the primary responsibility of the federal government, efforts to improve the route moved at a faster pace. The channel was widened, deepened and straightened. Where the bayou made an unusually sharp horseshoe bend, as at Harrisburg, dredges cut through the offending finger of land, shortening the route by a half mile or more during the process. At the wide bend above Harrisburg, where in 1837 Edward Auld had finally been able to swing his steamboat *Constitution* around after backing down the bayou all the way from Houston, the engineers cut into the banks with a will. They created an open expanse of water large enough for seagoing steamships to be turned around, like *Constitution*, to point their bows downstream again toward the Gulf of Mexico and the open sea. This turning basin, as it came to be called, marks the upstream end of the Houston Ship Channel to this day.

The first vessel officially to make use of the newly opened Houston Ship Channel arrived on August 22, 1915. She was the 312-foot-long *Satilla*, a freighter drawing 22 feet, with a cargo of general merchandise from New York. Although it would be many years before the Port of Houston would challenge Galveston's tonnage dominance in the deep-water shipping trade, the die had been cast. Today, almost a century after *Satilla*'s arrival, Houston ranks as one of the top ports in the United States, having long since eclipsed the island city in maritime trade.

The end of the Direct Navigation Company may be seen to mark the end of the Houston-Galveston packet trade, but it had effectively ended forty years before, with the retirement of the big passenger steamers *T.M. Bagby* and *Diana* and the transition of the company to an all-towing operation. In the decades after the Civil War, the company so thoroughly dominated the route that the Direct Navigation Company's operations effectively *were* the trade.

In many respects, the same forces that created Houston and the Buffalo Bayou packet trade in the 1830s and expanded and standardized it in the 1840s and 1850s ultimately doomed it to obsolescence in the 1870s and 1880s. The influx of settlers into Texas, mostly from the southern United States, during the period of the Texas Republic fueled the booming Buffalo Bayou trade. The "great commercial emporium" of Houston, with its unbridled mercantilism, drove the upstream trade, while Galveston's preeminence as the leading port in the region guaranteed rapid growth. The state's spectacular population growth during the middle years of the nineteenth century contributed heavily, as well. The disruptions and losses of the Civil War proved to be only a brief setback, and in the latter part of the 1860s, the steamboatmen and their investors seemed to be on track to reclaim the prominence they'd enjoyed in the previous decade.

But what they may not have realized immediately is that they, and Texas, had entered the modern era and were moving into what Twain would facetiously call the "Gilded Age" of unfettered capital expansion and consolidation. Texas was no longer the frontier, no longer the expansive destination for a continual stream of immigrants—both from other parts of the United States and from foreign countries—flooding into the state. While agricultural production, particularly of cotton, continued to grow, there were other, faster means of moving those products to transshipment points on Galveston Bay. Above all, there were the capitalists like Charles Morgan and Collis P. Huntington, whose financial grasp eventually consumed even powerful local interests like the Houston Direct Navigation Company and made them part of a truly national transportation network. The packet trade on Buffalo Bayou, in its fully realized form, only really lasted a few decades, but during that time it proved to be a vital and central link in the development of both Galveston and Houston, of Texas, and the American West.

APPENDIX

Steamboats Running on Buffalo Bayou

The following table lists steamboats that are known to have made at least one run on Buffalo Bayou. The list is generated from a variety of primary and secondary sources. This list is not meant to be comprehensive but is included instead to suggest the scope of the Buffalo Bayou trade and the vessels that maintained it.

Rig is abbreviated as SW=sidewheel, Stw=sternwheel and P=propeller. Tonnages are those listed in contemporary accounts and are calculated by different measures; they are provided here as a rough guide to the size of the vessel.

Vessels that are "abandoned" are generally those that have been taken out of service and dismantled; "off lists" indicates that a vessel dropped off the registry that year, and no further outcome is known.

Blank entries indicate unknown data.

Appendix

Name	Rig	Tons	Built	Where Built	Lost	Notes
A.S. Ruthven	SW	144	1860	Cincinatti, OH	1869	Abandoned, Trinity River
Albert Gallatin	SW	94	1839	Pittsburgh, PA	1841	Exploded
Alert (tug)	P					
Alice Blair	Stw		1890	Osceola, MO		
Ariel	SW	86	1825	New York, NY	1830	Abandoned, San Jacinto River
Arizona	Stw	253	1857	Belle Vernon, PA	1867	Abandoned
Bagdad		225				
Bayou City	SW		1859	Jeffersonville, IN	1865?	Exploded 1860; rebuilt. Confederate service, 1861–65.
Belle Sulphur	SW				1862	Wrecked
Betty Powell	SW	166	1854	Matagorda, TX	1859	Burned
Billow	SW	141	1846	Burlington, OH	1852	Abandoned
Branch T. Archer						
Brighton	SW	93	1836	Pittsburgh, PA	1841	Abandoned

Appendix

Name	Rig	Tons	Built	Where Built	Lost	Notes
Buck (tug)	P	10	1868	Galveston, TX	1873	
C.K. Hall		120			1871	Wrecked in storm
Caddo	Stw	188	1863	West Brownsville, PA	1871	Abandoned
Cash	Stw	57	1867	Buffalo Bayou, TX	1869	Abandoned
Charles Fowler			1871	New Albany, IN		Freight boat in H.D.N.Co.
Col. Stell	SW	198	1860	Pittsburgh, PA	1867	Also known as *J.D. Stelle*
Col. Woods	SW	134	1839	Brownsville, PA		Came to Texas 1844
Constitution	SW	262	1830	Cincinnati, OH	1838	Stranded at Matagorda, TX
Correo	SW	66	1836	New Albany, IN		Also known as *Gov. Smith*
Crescent (tug)	P	34	1867	New Albany, IN	1874	Abandoned
Crusader	SW	120	1836	Gallipolis, OH		Came to Texas 1838
Dayton	SW	111	1835	Pittsburgh, PA	1845	Exploded

APPENDIX

Name	Rig	Tons	Built	Where Built	Lost	Notes
Diana	SW	239	1858	Brownsville, PA	1863	Burned
Diana	SW	452	1870	Cincinnati, OH		Cut down to a barge, c. 1879
Dime	SW	33	1859	Louisville, KY		Confederate service
Edward Burleson	SW	179	1839	Marietta, OH		Orig. name *Victoria*
Ellen P. Frankland	SW?					
Emblem	SW	120	1836	Cincinnati, OH	1839	Foundered
Era No. 3	Stw	144	1858	Freedon, PA		Confederate service
Farmer	SW	158	1849	Brownsville, PA	1853	Exploded
Franklin Pierce	SW	348	1853	Covington, KY	1855	Burned. Later named *Texana*
Friend	SW	71		Cincinnati, OH		
Grand Bay	Stw	135	1857	Mobile, AL		Confederate service
Grapeshot	Stw	179	1855	Louisville, KY	1858	Burned
Henry A. Jones	Stw		1869	Pittsburgh, PA	1873	Burned

Appendix

Name	Rig	Tons	Built	Where Built	Lost	Notes
Island City	SW	245	1856	Brownsville, PA		Confederate service
J.H. Whitelaw	SW	439	1865	Beardstown, IL	1871	
Jeff Davis						Confederate service
John F. Carr						Confederate service
Lady Byron	SW	90	1830	Steubenville, OH	1844	Snagged. Earlier named *Trinity*.
Laura	SW	65	1835	Louisville, KY		
Leonidas	SW	97	1834	Cincinnati, OH		Formerly *Don Pedro*; later *Sam Houston*
Lizzie	SW	429	1871	Jeffersonville, IN	1880?	
Lone Star						Confederate service
Louise (tug)	P					Sunk in 1900 storm
Lucy Gwinn	Stw	152	1859	Freedom, PA		Confederate service
Mary Conley	SW	162	1865	Mobile, AL	1873	Snagged, Trinity River

Appendix

Name	Rig	Tons	Built	Where Built	Lost	Notes
Mary Hill	SW	234	1855	TX		Confederate service
Maryland	SW	121	1837	Pittsburgh, PA	1843	Abandoned
McLean						Racing *Billow* in 1848. Possibly *Judge McLean*, built 1844 at Louisville.
Mustang	SW		1842	Galveston, TX?	1843	Sank. Orig. built as Galv.-Virginia Pt. ferry.
Neptune	Stw	214	1852	Brownsville, PA	1858	Off lists
Neptune No. 2	SW	257	1859	Brownsville, TX	1863	Confederate service; abandoned and salvaged after Battle of Galveston.
Nick Hill	Stw	97	1851	Buffalo Bayou	1853	Stranded, Trinity River. Also blew up boilers on first trip, 1851, but repaired.
Ontario (tug)	P	8	1866	Buffalo, NY	1929	Abandoned
Oriole	SW	110	1840	Cincinnati, OH		Came to Texas 1846
Patrick Henry	SW	161	1840	Cincinnati, OH	1850	Foundered

APPENDIX

Name	Rig	Tons	Built	Where Built	Lost	Notes
Reliance	SW	156	1845	Cincinnati, OH	1854	Off lists
Rob Roy						Confederate service
Rodney	SW	99	1836	Jeffersonville, IN	1840	Sank
Roebuck	SW	164	1857	Brownsville, PA		Confederate service
Royal Arch	P	65	1864	Maumee, OH		
Rufus Putnam	SW	98	1835	Marietta, OH		
S.J. Lee	Stw	176	1866	Galveston, TX	1873	Iron hull. Stranded at Brownsville, TX
Sam Houston						Running in 1830s. Original name?
San Antonio	SW	127	1854	Freedom, PA		
San Jacinto	SW	71	1853	Houston, TX	1855	Abandoned
San Jacinto						Running c. 1838
Shreveport						Confederate service

Appendix

Name	Rig	Tons	Built	Where Built	Lost	Notes
Silver Cloud	Stw	236	1862	Brownsville, PA	1866	Snagged on Buffalo Bayou 1866. USN "Tinclad" No. 28.
Spartan	SW	99	1844	Burch Creek, OH		Came to Texas c, 1845
St. Clair	Stw	203	1862	Belle Vernon, PA	1869	Off lists; USN "Tinclad" No. 19.
Sunflower	SW	105	1857	Louisville, KY	1867	Wrecked
Superior (tug)	P	14	1866	Buffalo, NY	1877	Abandoned
T.M. Bagby	SW	508	1868	Louisville, KY	c. 1876	Dismantled
Trinity	SW	88	1839	Cincinnati, OH		Former *Grecian*; later *Lady Byron*
Uncle Ben	SW	155	1856	Buffalo, NY		Confederate service
Victoria	SW	85	1837	Brownsville, PA	1843	Abandoned
Warsaw	SW	146	1833	Wheeling, VA	1839	Converted to warehouse and hotel at Galveston in Jan. 1839
Wren						Running on Buffalo Bayou 1871–73. Possibly built Louisville 1862.
Yellow Stone	SW	144	1831	Louisville, KY		Possibly returned to U.S. from Texas

NOTES

Chapter 1. Arroyo Cibolo

1. The Spanish did establish a landing at El Copano, in what is now Refugio County, in the eighteenth century. Copano was used sporadically for the resupply of the Spanish missions and presidio near Goliad. It was not until after the Texas Revolution, however, that Copano began to grow as a community in its own right. Guthrie, *Texas Forgotten Ports*, 6–10.
2. Meinig, *Imperial Texas*, 26–27.
3. Quoted in Hogan, *Texas Republic*, 57.
4. Olmstead, *Journey Through Texas*, 55.
5. Hogan, *Texas Republic*, 68.
6. Lide, "Navigation on Buffalo Bayou," 2.
7. *Houston Chronicle*, May 2, 1929, 26; Page, *Prairiedom*, 97.
8. Page, *Prairiedom*, 99–100.
9. Clopper, *American Family*, 176.
10. Page, *Prairiedom*, 86.
11. Young, *True Stories of Old Houston*, 37–8.
12. Audubon, *Life of John James Audubon*, 410–11; Works Progress Administration, *Ship Registers and Enrollments*, Vol. III, 55.
13. Domenech, *Missionary Adventures in Texas*, 24.
14. Ibid.
15. Hunter, *Steamboats on the Western Rivers*, 192–3.
16. Sibley, *Port of Houston*, 17–8.

17. Weinberger, "Houston Ship Channel," 46.
18. Alperin, *Custodians of the Coast*, 92; Guthrie, *Texas Forgotten Ports*, 220.
19. Holland, *America's Lighthouses*, 152.
20. Houstoun, *Texas and the Gulf*, 146–7.
21. *Galveston Daily News*, October 6, 1871, 3; *Galveston Daily News*, October 10, 1871, 3; Hayes, *Galveston: A History*, 725.
22. Guthrie, *Forgotten Ports*, vol. II, 222.
23. Despite improvements made since 1900 that have greatly reduced the loss of life and property, Galveston remains under threat from such events. Hurricane Ike, in 2008, brought with it a fourteen-foot storm surge that flooded about three-quarters of the buildings on the island.
24. Swenson, "A Journey from Sweden to Texas in 1867," 68–9.
25. Houstoun, *Texas and the Gulf*, Vol. I, 186–9. *New York* was a 365-ton seagoing steamship that normally ran between Galveston and New Orleans. She foundered in the Gulf of Mexico in September 1846, with the loss of seventeen lives. Mitchell, *Merchant Steam Vessels*, 285.

Chapter 2. Snags

26. Hogan, "Henry Austin," 186–9.
27. Mitchell, *Merchant Steam Vessels*, 13.
28. Hogan, "Henry Austin," 190–1.
29. Ibid., 192–3.
30. Francaviglia, *From Sail to Steam*, 100–01.
31. Jordan, *Lone Star Navy*, 40–1; Works Progress Administration, *Ship Registers and Enrollments, Vol. III*, 30.
32. Sibley, *Port of Houston: A History*, 31–3.
33. *Telegraph and Texas Register*, October 18, 1836.
34. Ibid.
35. Works Progress Administration, *Ship Registers and Enrollments*, Vol. III, 121.
36. Lubbock, *Six Decades in Texas*, 46.
37. Ibid.; *Telegraph and Texas Register*, January 27, 1837.
38. Lubbock, *Six Decades in Texas*, 54.
39. *Telegraph and Texas Register*, April 11, 1837, February 28, 1837, 4.
40. Sibley, *Lone Stars and State Gazettes*, 88.
41. *Telegraph and Texas Register*, May 2, 1837.
42. Works Progress Administration, *Ship Registers and Enrollments*, Vol. III, 48–49.

43. *Baltimore Gazette and Daily Advertiser*, September 16, 1831, June 17, 1833.
44. *Telegraph and Texas Register*, June 3, 1837.
45. Hayes, *Galveston: A History*, 319.
46. *Philadelphia Inquirer*, December 11, 1839.
47. Young, *True Stories of Old Houston*, 55. The natural contours of Constitution Bend were wiped away in later dredging and widening of the Houston Ship Channel, but it lay just about exactly where the Port of Houston's turning basin is today.
48. Lide, "The History of Navigation," 53; *Houston Telegraph and Texas Register*, December 29, 1838.
49. *Houston Telegraph and Texas Register*, July 21, 1838.
50. Lide., "The History of Navigation," 59; *Houston Telegraph and Texas Register*, December 29, 1838.
51. Lide, "The History of Navigation," 45.
52. Ibid., 50.
53. Ibid., 65.
54. *Houston Telegraph and Texas Register*, December 29, 1838.
55. Dresel, *Houston Journal*, 29–31.
56. *Telegraph and Texas Register*, October 18, 1836.

Chapter 3. Gone to Texas

57. U.S. Census of 1860, Ward 4, Houston, Harris County, Texas, 151.; Works Progress Administration, *Ship Registers and Enrollments, Vol. III*, 187.
58. Juliet M. Sterrett Manlove to Juliet Day, March 24, 1838. Courtesy Bill Day, Minneapolis, Minnesota.
59. Ibid.
60. Works Progress Administration, *Ship Registers and Enrollments, Vol. III*, 187.
61. *Telegraph and Texas Register*, January 16, 1839, 4.
62. Lide, "The History of Navigation," 70.
63. Ibid.,111.
64. Black, *Notable Women Authors*, 90–91.
65. Black, *Notable Women Authors*, 91.
66. *Telegraph and Texas Register*, March 22, 1843, 2.
67. Houstoun, *Texas and the Gulf*, Vol. I, 255–63.
68. Houstoun, *Texas and the Gulf*, Vol. II, 178; *Telegraph and Texas Register*, February 1, 1843.

69. Works Progress Administration, *Ship Registers and Enrollments*, Vol. III, 59; Houstoun, *Texas and the Gulf*, Vol. II, 179.
70. Houstoun, *Texas and the Gulf*, Vol. II, 180.
71. Ibid., 181; Ibid., 183.
72. Ibid., 183.
73. Ibid., 208.
74. Ibid., 209.
75. Ibid., 211.
76. Ibid., 214–15.
77. Ibid., 234–35.
78. Louis C. Hunter, *Steamboats on the Western Rivers*, 336–37.
79. Weinberger, "Houston Ship Channel," 46.
80. *Telegraph and Texas Register*, January 3, 1844; *Galveston Civilian and Gazette Weekly*, May 4, 1858; *Telegraph and Texas Register*, November 13, 1844. *Dayton* would soon meet her own violent end. Chartered by the U.S. Army's Quartermaster Department to ferry troops between Mustang Island and Corpus Christi during the war with Mexico, the little steamer blew up her boilers at Aransas Pass, Texas, in September 1845. At least ten persons were killed, and several others, including her master at the time, Captain West, were severely scalded. *Dayton* became one of the worst early maritime disasters in Texas. *Houston Telegraph*, September 24, 1845; Mitchell, *Merchant Steam Vessels*, 255.

Chapter 4. Years of Growth and Stability

81. *Telegraph and Texas Register*, December 5, 1851.
82. Hunter, *Steamboats on the Western Rivers*, 405.
83. Lide, "The History of Navigation," 112.
84. Twain, *Life on the Mississippi*, 163.
85. *Houston Telegraph*, June 1, 1848, 2.
86. *Telegraph and Texas Register*, April 18, 1851.
87. Sibley, *The Port of Houston*, 71; Hayes, *Galveston: A History*, 724–5.
88. *Tri-Weekly News*, March 29, 1853, April 5, 1853; Clipping from unknown periodical, April 23, 1853, Galveston and Texas History Center, Rosenberg Library, Galveston.
89. Sibley, *The Port of Houston*, 71.
90. Clipping from an unknown periodical, April, 23, 1853, Galveston and Texas History Center, Rosenberg Library, Galveston; Hunter, *Steamboats on the Western Rivers*, 448–50; Stampp, *The Peculiar Institution*, 414–15. One

of the slaves killed in the accident belonged to Capt. Delesdernier, himself an old Buffalo Bayou pilot.
91. Mitchell, *Merchant Steam Vessels*, 18; Way, *Way's Packet Directory*, 40; *Galveston Civilian and Gazette Weekly*, September 25, 1860, 3; *Colorado Citizen*, September 29, 1860, 2.
92. *Galveston Civilian and Gazette Weekly*, October 2, 1860, 3.
93. *Galveston Civilian and Gazette Weekly*, October 2, 1860, 1; *Galveston Civilian and Gazette Weekly*, October 16, 1860, 1. After losing his license as a steamboat engineer, Numa Whitson continued to work at his trade on shore. In the mid-1870s he moved to Coryell County, Texas, where he founded a settlement named for him, southeast of Waco.
94. Hunter, *Steamboats on the Western Rivers*, 338–39; Fornell, *The Galveston Era*, 30–31; Moody, *Stagecoach West*, 84–85.
95. Fornell, *The Galveston Era*, 32.
96. *Galveston Civilian and Gazette*, May 4, 1858, 1. The newspaper's claim that Sterrett had, in nineteen years on the route, made the passage between Galveston and Houston some four thousand times averages out to about three one-way trips in every five days. Although the exact number cannot be known, the newspaper's estimate in Sterrett's case is entirely plausible.
97. Advertising broadside, n.d., Houston Metropolitan Research Center, Houston Public Library.
98. Quoted in Stuart, "Texas Steamboat Days," 31–32.
99. Ibid., 52–54.
100. *Galveston Tri-Weekly News*, February 19, 1856.
101. *Galveston Daily News*, June 19, 1927, 22.
102. Muir, "Railroads Come to Houston," 55; Houston *City Directory*, 1870–71, Houston Metropolitan Research Center, Houston Public Library; *Houston Republic*, January 30, 1858; U.S. Census of 1850; Ward 4, Houston, Harris County, Texas, 30; U.S. Census of 1860; Ward 4, Houston, Harris County, Texas, 151.

Chapter 5. The Texas Marine Department

103. U.S. Census of 1860; Ward 3, Houston, Harris County, Texas, 119.
104. Young, *True Stories of Old Houston*, 214.
105. Ibid., 214.
106. Cotham, *Battle on the Bay*, 8.
107. Hayes, *Galveston: A History*, 751.

108. Underwood, *Waters of Discord*, 23–24.
109. *Galveston Civilian and Gazette Weekly*, July 9, 1861.
110. Hayes, *Galveston: A History*, 750.
111. "Agreement of Houston Navigation Company regarding the charter of vessels for the Confederate Government," in *Official Records of the Union and Confederate Navies in the War of the Rebellion* (hereafter cited as "*Official Records*"), series I, vol. 16 (Washington: Government Printing Office, 1903), 841. *Neptune No. 2* was the second *Neptune* operated by the Houston Navigation Company. Although this second boat was later referred to by the single name *Neptune*, I have used her full, original name throughout to keep the two boats' careers distinct.
112. Confederate Citizens' file, "John H. Sterrett," Confederate Papers Relating to Citizens or Business Firms. RG 109 NARA M346, Catalog No. 2133274, p. 8
113. Ibid., 13.
114. "Agreement of Houston Navigation Company regarding the charter of vessels for the Confederate Government," in *Official Records of the Union and Confederate Navies in the War of the Rebellion* (hereafter cited as "*Official Records*"), series I, vol. 16 (Washington: Government Printing Office, 1903), 841; "Log of the C.S.S. *Bayou City*, Master P.F. Appel, C.S. Navy, Commanding," Ibid., 860–69.
115. John H. Sterrett Confederate Citizens' file, 4; C. Blakeman Confederate Citizens' file, 3.
116. Cotham, *Battle on the Bay*, 63–63.
117. Ibid., 105–06.
118. Ibid., 106.
119. Lubbock, *Six Decades in Texas*, 429–30.
120. Cotham, *Battle of the Bay*, 124.
121. Ibid., 110–111; Hayes, *Galveston: A History*, 551.
122. Hayes, *Galveston: A History*, 551–52; Cotham, *Battle on the Bay*, 112.
123. Hayes, *Galveston: A History*, 552.
124. *Dallas Morning News*, January 2, 1903, 3; Tiling, *History of the German Element in Texas from 1820-1850*, 122.
125. Franklin, *Battle of Galveston*, 8.
126. Ibid., 9.
127. David D. Porter to Gustavus V. Fox, "Letter from Rear-Admiral Porter, U.S. Navy, to the Assistant Secretary of the Navy, requesting lights for the vessels in James River," November 19, 1864, in *Official Records*, series I, vol. 11 (Washington: Government Printing Office, 1900), 77.

128. "Report of Commodore H.H. Bell, West Gulf Blockading Squadron," in *Official Records*, series I, vol. 20 (Washington: Government Printing Office, 1905), 761.
129. Hearn, *Admiral David Glasgow Farragut*, 183–84.
130. *Galveston Weekly News*, February 11, 1863, June 10, 1863; *Houston Telegraph*, November 9, 1863.
131. John H. Sterrett to Edmund P Turner, "*Report of superintendent of transports regarding the vessels of the Marine Department, October 27, 1863. Official Records*, series I, vol. 20 (Washington: Government Printing Office, 1905), 845-46.
132. Compiled from Appendices 17 and 18 of Wise, *Lifeline of the Confederacy*, 272–75.
133. D.G. Farragut to T. Bailey, "*Letter from Rear-Admiral Farragut, U. S. Navy, to Rear-Admiral Bailey, U. S. Navy, referring to the captured steamer Donegal, or Austin.," Official Records*, series I, vol. 21 (Washington: Government Printing Office, 1906), 334–35.
134. *Galveston Weekly News*, April 26, 1865.
135. Cotham, *Battle of the Bay*, 182–83.

Chapter 6. Rebuilding

136. *Galveston News*, June 17, 1865; Hayes, *Galveston: A History*, 643.
137. *Galveston News*, September 2, 1865.
138. Ibid., October 18, 1865.
139. Mitchell, *Merchant Steam Vessels*, 191; Way, *Way's Packet Directory*, 409.
140. Mitchell, *Merchant Steam Vessels*, 199; Way, *Way's Packet Directory*, 425.
141. Sherman, *Sherman's Selected Correspondence*, 585–87.
142. Critchell, *Recollections of a Fire Insurance Man*, 37–38.
143. *Galveston Weekly News*, November 8, 1865.
144. Houston City Directory, 1866, Houston Metropolitan Research Center, Houston Public Library; Farrar, Story of Buffalo Bayou, 12; Mitchell, *Merchant Steam Vessels*, 297.
145. Farrar, *Story of Buffalo Bayou*, 11.
146. Baughman, *Charles Morgan*, 216.
147. Swenson, "Journey from Sweden to Texas," 68–69.
148. McComb, *Houston: A History*, 33; Stuart, "Texas Steamboat Days," 64.
149. Stuart, "Texas Steamboat Days," 67–68.
150. *Galveston Daily News*, May 3, 1866.

151. United States Bureau of Engineers, *Report of the Chief of Engineers* (Washington: Government Printing Office, 1871), 537
152. Way, *Way's Packet Directory*, 28, 232, 421.
153. *Galveston Daily News*, August 12, 1870.
154. Farrar, *Story of Buffalo Bayou*, 11.
155. *Galveston News*, January 31, 1873, January 1, 1873; Stuart, "Texas Steamboat Days," 66.

Chapter 7. Morgan Moves In

156. *Galveston Daily News*, October 9, 1868; *Galveston Daily News*, March 2, 1876.
157. *Galveston Daily News*, July 5, 1871; Baughman, *Charles Morgan*, 205–07.
158. Hayes, *History of the Island*, 780.
159. *Galveston News*, February 15, 1873; Hayes, *History of the Island*, 725.
160. Malsch, *Indianola*, 213; *Galveston Daily News*, May 7, 1874.
161. Weinberger, "Houston Ship Channel," 87.
162. Francaviglia, *From Sail to Steam*, 261–62. Morgan's creation, the Ship Channel Company, appears to be the first use of the term "ship channel" for this improved waterway.
163. Weinberger, "Houston Ship Channel," 89–90.
164. Francaviglia, *From Sail to Steam*, 262; Weinberger, "Houston Ship Channel," 90.
165. Quoted in Weinberger, "Houston Ship Channel," 91.
166. *Galveston Daily News*, February 16, 1877.
167. Ibid., September 26, 1876, September 8, 1876, 7.
168. Ibid., November 26, 1875, 4.
169. U.S. Census of 1850; Ward 4, Houston, Harris County, Texas, 30; U.S. Census of 1860; Ward 4, Houston, Harris County, Texas, 151; U.S. Census of 1870; Ward 3, Houston, Harris County, Texas, 35.
170. *Galveston Daily News*, December 7, 1875.
171. *Galveston Daily News*, May 2, 1876.
172. *Galveston Daily News*, June 19, 1879; clipping from an unidentified Houston newspaper, June 19, 1879, author's collection.

Chapter 8. The Final Years

173. Both tugs were launched at Buffalo, New York, in 1866. *Superior* remained in service until 1877; *Ontario* survived until being abandoned in 1929. Mitchell, *Merchant Steam Vessels*, 164; Ibid., 206.
174. United States Bureau of Engineers, *Report of the Chief of Engineers* (Washington: Government Printing Office, 1871), 537
175. *Galveston Daily News*, October 31, 1882, 7.
176. Ibid., June 19, 1927, 22; Way, *Way's Packet Directory*, 441; *Galveston Daily News*, October 14, 1883, 8.
177. *Galveston Daily News*, November 13, 1880, 7.
178. Sibley, *The Port of Houston*, 103.
179. *Galveston Daily News*, December 3, 1883, 7.
180. Sibley, *The Port of Houston*, 103.
181. Ibid., 105; Ibid., 108.
182. Ibid., 108.
183. Baughman, *Charles Morgan*, 218–19.
184. Sibley, *The Port of Houston*, 105–06.
185. Baughman, *Charles Morgan*, 232–35.
186. Weinberger, "The Houston Ship Channel," 161.
187. Alperin, *Custodians of the Coast*, 97–98; Sibley, *The Port of Houston*, 110.
188. *Houston Daily Post*, September 14, 1900, September 15, 1900.
189. Works Progress Administration, *Houston: A History and Guide* (Houston: Anson Jones Press, 1942), 136.
190. *Galveston Daily News*, August 17, 1915; *San Antonio Light*, August 27, 1915; *Galveston Daily News*, February 8, 1916, September 29, 1920.

BIBLIOGRAPHY

BOOKS

Alperin, Lynn M. *Custodians of the Coast: History of the United States Army Engineers at Galveston*. Galveston, TX: U.S. Army Corps of Engineers, 1977.

Audubon, John James. *The Life of John James Audubon, the Naturalist*. Lucy Green Bakewell Audubon, ed. New York: Putnam, 1894.

Bates, Alan L. *The Western Rivers Engine Room Cyclopædium*. Louisville, KY: Cyclopedium Press, 1996.

———. *The Western Rivers Steamboat Cyclopædium*. Leona, NJ: Hustle Press, 1968.

Baughman, James P. *Charles Morgan and the Development of Southern Transportation*. Nashville, TN: Vanderbilt University, 1968.

Black, C. *Notable Women Authors of the Day*. London: MacLaren and Company, 1906.

Clopper, Edward Nicholas. *An American Family: Its Ups and Downs Through Eight Generations in New Amsterdam, New York, Pennsylvania, Maryland, Ohio, and Texas, from 1650 to 1880*. New York: Standard Printing and Publ. Co., 1950.

Cotham, Edward T., Jr. *Battle on the Bay: The Civil War Struggle for Galveston*. Austin: University of Texas, 1998.

Critchell, Robert S. *Recollections of a Fire Insurance Man*. Chicago: McClurg and Co., 1909.

Bibliography

Domenech, Emmanuel. *Missionary Adventures in Texas and Mexico: A Personal Narrative of Six Years' Sojourn in Those Regions*. London: Longman, Brown, Green, Longmans and Roberts, 1858.

Dresel, Gustav. *Gustav Dresel's Houston Journal: Adventures in North America and Texas, 1837–1841*. Trans. by Max Freund. Austin: University of Texas Press, 1954.

Farrar, R.M. *The Story of Buffalo Bayou and the Houston Ship Channel*. Houston, TX: Chamber of Commerce, 1926.

Fornell, Earl Wesley. *The Galveston Era: The Texas Crescent on the Eve of Secession*. Austin: University of Texas Press, 1976.

Francaviglia, Richard V. *From Sail to Steam: Four Centuries of Texas Maritime History, 1500–1900*. Austin: University of Texas, 1998.

Franklin, Robert M. *The Battle of Galveston*. Galveston, TX: San Luis Press, 1975.

Guthrie, Keith. *Texas Forgotten Ports*. Austin, TX: Eakin Press, 1988.

———. *Texas Forgotten Ports, vol. II*. Austin, TX: Eakin Press, 1993.

Hayes, Charles Waldo. *Galveston: A History of the Island and the City*. Austin, TX: Jenkins Garrett Press, 1974.

Hearn, Chester G. *Admiral David Glasgow Farragut: The Civil War Years*. Annapolis, MD: Naval Institute Press, 1998.

Hogan, William Ransom. *The Texas Republic: A Social and Economic History*. Austin: University of Texas, 1969.

Holland, Francis Ross, Jr. *America's Lighthouses: An Illustrated History*. New York: Dover, 1988.

Houston City Directory, 1866, Houston Metropolitan Research Center, Houston Public Library.

Houston City Directory, 1870–71, Houston Metropolitan Research Center, Houston Public Library.

Houstoun, Matilda Charlotte. *Texas and the Gulf of Mexico, or Yachting in the New World*, Vol. I. London: John Murray, 1844.

———. *Texas and the Gulf of Mexico, or Yachting in the New World*, Vol. II. London: John Murray, 1844.

Huber, Leonard V. *Advertisements of Lower Mississippi River Steamboats, 1812–1920*. West Barrington, Rhode Island: Steamship Historical Society of America, 1959.

Hunter, Louis C. *Steamboats on the Western Rivers*. New York: Dover, 1993.

Jordan, Jonathan W. *Lone Star Navy: Texas, the Fight for the Gulf of Mexico, and the Shaping of the American West*. Washington, D.C.: Potomac Books, 2007.

Kane, Adam I. *The Western River Steamboat*. College Station: Texas A&M Press, 2004.

BIBLIOGRAPHY

King, Edward. *The Southern States of North America.* London: Blackie and Son, 1875.

Lubbock, Francis Richard. *Six Decades in Texas or, Memoirs of Francis Richard Lubbock, Governor of Texas in War-Time, 1861-63, A Personal Experience in Business, War and Politics.* C.W. Raines, ed. Austin, TX: Ben C. Jones & Co., 1900.

Malsch, Brownson. *Indianola: The Mother of Western Texas.* Austin, TX: State House Press, 1988.

McComb, David G. *Houston: A History.* Austin: University of Texas Press, 1981.

Meinig, D.W. *Imperial Texas: An Interpretive Essay in Cultural Geography.* Austin: University of Texas Press, 1969.

Mitchell, C. Bradford, ed. *Merchant Steam Vessels of the United States, 1790-1868 (The Lytle-Holdcamper List).* Staten Island, New York: Steamship Historical Society of America, 1975.

Moody, Ralph. *Stagecoach West.* New York: Promontory Press, 1967.

Olmstead, Frederick Law. *A Journey Through Texas.* New York: Dix, Edwards & Co, 1857.

Page, Frederick Benjamin. *Prairiedom: Rambles and Scrambles in Texas or New Estrémadura.* New York: Payne and Burgess, 1845.

Paine, Lincoln P. *Ships of the World: An Historical Encyclopedia.* Boston: Houghton Mifflin, 1997.

Sherman, William T. *Sherman's Selected Correspondence of the Civil War.* Brooks D. Simpson and Jean V. Berlin, eds. Chapel Hill: University of North Carolina Press, 1999.

Sibley, Marilyn McAdams. *Lone Stars and State Gazettes: Texas Newspapers Before the Civil War.* College Station: Texas A&M Press, 1983.

———. *The Port of Houston: A History.* Austin: The University of Texas Press, 1968.

Stampp, Kenneth M. *The Peculiar Institution: Slavery in the Ante-Bellum South.* New York: Alfred A. Knopf, 1972.

Tiling, Moritz Philipp Georg. *History of the German Element in Texas from 1820-1850, and Historical Sketches of the German Texas Singers' League and Houston Turnverein from 1853-1913.* Houston: Moritz Tiling, 1913.

Twain, Mark. *Life on the Mississippi.* Montreal: Dawson Brothers, 1883.

Underwood, Rodman L. *Waters of Discord: The Union Blockade of Texas During the Civil War.* Jefferson, NC: McFarland and Company, 2003.

Way, Frederick, Jr. *Way's Packet Directory, 1848-1983.* Athens: Ohio University Press, 1984.

Bibliography

Wise, Stephen R. *Lifeline of the Confederacy: Blockade Running During the Civil War*. Columbia: University of South Carolina Press, 1988

Works Progress Administration. *Houston: A History and Guide*. Houston, TX: Anson Jones Press, 1942.

Young, S.O. *True Stories of Old Houston and Houstonians*. Galveston, TX: Oscar Springer, 1913.

Journal Articles

Hogan, William Ransom. "Henry Austin." *Southwestern Historical Quarterly* 37 (1934): 185–214.

Muir, Andrew Forest. "Railroads Come to Houston." *Southwestern Historical Quarterly* 64 (1961): 42–63.

Swenson, Johannes. "A Journey from Sweden to Texas in 1867." Trans. by Carl T. Weldon. *Southwestern Historical Quarterly* 62 (1958): 68–9.

Unpublished Works

Lide, Frances. "The History of Navigation on Buffalo Bayou, 1836-1845." Unpublished masters thesis, The University of Texas, 1937.

Stuart, Ben C. "Texas Steamboat Days: Annals of Steam Transportation on Inland Waters from the Colonial Period to the End of the Era, with a List of Boats and River Men." Unpublished typescript, Galveston and Texas History Center, Rosenberg Library, Galveston, Texas.

Weinberger, A.L. "The History and Development of the Houston Ship Channel and the Port of Houston" Unpublished masters thesis, the University of Texas, 1940.

Public Records

Confederate Papers Relating to Citizens or Business Firms, 1861–65 ("Citizens Files"). NARA M346., National Archives and Records Administration.

Bibliography

Official Records of the Union and Confederate Navies in the War of the Rebellion, 21 vols. Washington: Government Printing Office, 1900-1906.

United States Bureau of Engineers, *Report of the Chief of Engineers*. Washington: Government Printing Office, 1871.

United States Decennial Census of 1850.

United States Decennial Census of 1860.

United States Decennial Census of 1870.

Works Progress Administration, *Ship Registers and Enrollments of the Port of New Orleans, Louisiana*, Vol. I, 1804-1820. New Orleans: Louisiana State University, 1942.

Works Progress Administration, *Ship Registers and Enrollments of the Port of New Orleans, Louisiana*, Vol. II, 1821-1830. New Orleans: Louisiana State University, 1942.

Works Progress Administration, *Ship Registers and Enrollments of the Port of New Orleans, Louisiana*, Vol. III, 1831-1840. New Orleans: Louisiana State University, 1942.

Newspapers

Baltimore Gazette and Daily Advertiser
Galveston Civilian and Gazette
Galveston Daily News
Galveston News
Galveston Tri-Weekly News
Galveston Weekly News
Houston Chronicle
Houston Daily Post
Houston Telegraph
Houston Telegraph and Texas Register
Philadelphia Inquirer
San Antonio Light
Telegraph and Texas Register

BIBLIOGRAPHY

Archival Sources and Clippings

Manlove, Juliet M. Sterrett to Juliet Day, March 24, 1838. Courtesy Bill Day, Minneapolis, Minnesota.
Vertical files, Galveston and Texas History Center, Rosenberg Library, Galveston.
Vertical files, Houston Metropolitan Research Center, Houston Public Library, Houston.

INDEX

A

Alden, James 65
Allen, Augustus Chapman 30
Allen Brothers 38
  Charter *Constitution* 34
  Charter *Laura* 32
  Promotion of Houston 31
Allen, John Kirby 30
Anaconda Plan 65
Annexation of Texas 47
Ariel 28
Arizona 83, 86
A.S. Ruthven 83
Audubon, John James 16
Auld, Edward 36, 47
  Later career of 36
Austin, Henry 30
  Background of 27
  Legacy of 30
Austin, Stephen F. 12, 27
  Austin's Colony 12, 13

B

barges
  Houston Direct Navigation Co., described 104

Battle of Mobile Bay 81
Bayou City 65, 66, 67, 72, 75, 76
  believed to be a ram 79
  cause of boiler explosion 56
  fitted out as a "cottonclad" 71
  rams *Harriet Lane* 76
  rebuilt after explosion 56
  selected as "cottonclad" 69
  sold to Confederate government 80
Bell, Henry H. 79
Billow 52
Bird Key 82
Blakeman, Curtis 52, 68, 84, 86, 96
Blockade running at Galveston 82
Bolivar Roads 24
Branch T. Archer 36
Brazos River 11, 45, 93
Bryan, Captain 41
Buffalo Bayou
  alligators in 14, 16
  currents and tides on 16
  fish and acquatic life in 14
  naming of 13
  vegetation on 14, 17, 44
  wildlife 13
Buffalo Bayou, Brazos & Colorado Railroad 89

Index

C

Camino Real 11
Charles Fowler 89, 92, 93, 96
Christian, S.P. 97
C.K. Hall 23
Clinton, Texas 100
  new cotton presses built at 106
Clopper, Nicholas 19
Clopper's Bar 19, 37, 46, 49
Colorado River 11
Constitution 36, 47
  passage up Buffalo Bayou 35
Constitution Bend 36
  becomes ship channel turning basin 112
Cook, Joseph Jarvis 68, 73
  failed assault on Kuhn's Wharf 74
Correo 36, 37, 38
Crocker, Charles 109
Crusader 16
Curly, John 56

D

Davis, A.J. 37
Dayton 43, 45, 46
  under Sterrett's command 47
DeBray, Xavier 69
Delesdernier, John 42
Denbigh 82
Diana 65, 82, 89, 92, 93
  cut down for a barge 105
  description of 92
Direct Navigation Company
  ceases operations 111
  operated at a loss 111
direct transfer 87, 88
Dolphin 25, 26, 42, 46
Domenech, Emmanuel 17
Dresel, Gustav 38

E

Ellen P. Frankland 22
Emblem 41

F

fares 37, 59, 92, 93
  fares "rate fights" 60
Farragut, David Glasgow 79
Ferguson, William 85
food 44, 45, 46, 60
Forrest, James 56
Forrest, Nathan Bedford 85
Forshey, Caleb 69
Fowler, Charles 98
Fox, Gustavus 79
Friend 36
fuel 51, 88, 96

G

Galveston
  description of 43
Galveston Bay
  description of 22
  weather on 22
Galveston, Houston & Henderson Railroad 89, 92
  becomes primary cotton carrier 92
Galveston Island
  description of 24
Galveston Wharf Company 87, 98, 99, 100, 108
gambling 61
  three-card-monte 61
Gordon, Dave S. 96
Green, Tom 71

H

Harriet Lane 75
Harrisburg 89
Harris, Edward 16
Hébert, Paul Octave 66, 68, 80
Henry A. Jones 89, 92, 96
  burned 98
  financial loss to company 98
Hillendahl 14
Hopkins, Mark 109

INDEX

Houston
  description of 34
Houston and Galveston Navigation
    Company 49, 52, 56
Houston and Texas Central Railroad
  absorbed by Southern Pacific 109
Houston Cotton Exchange 105, 106
Houston Direct Navigation Company
    103
  absorbed by Southern Pacific 109
  ends passenger service 104
  expanded alliance with Morgan 101
  expands alliances with Morgan
    interests 98
  founded 86
  partners with railroads 89
Houston Navigation Company 57, 65,
    86
  fares 59
  offers charter to Confederacy 66
  offices of 62
  organized 56
Houstoun, Captain M. C. 42
Houstoun, Matilda Charlotte 25, 42
Huntington, Collis P. 109

I

Irvin, Isaiah 56

J

Jesse, Edward 42
J.H. Whitelaw 89, 92
John F. Carr 72
Juno 110

K

Kellersberger, Julius 68
Kelsey, D.S. 43, 47
Kelsey, Mrs. 45
King Cotton strategy 65
Kuhn's Wharf 74

L

Laffite, Jean 24
Lark 82
Laura 32, 36
  passage up Buffalo Bayou 33
Lawrence, F.G. 36
Law, Richard 78
  court-martialed 79
Lea, Edward 77
Leonidas 36
Lizzie 89, 92
Lone Star 83
Louise 106, 110
Lubbock, Francis Richard 34
Lucy Gwinn 72

M

Maffitt, John Newland 82
Magruder, John Bankhead 68, 72
  fires first gun at Battle of Galveston
    74
  selected steamers for Galveston attack
    69
  strengthens Galveston's defenses 80
mail contracts 47, 59
  "bottlenecks" at Galveston 57
  use of private couriers 57
Mary Hill 67, 83
McCormick, Michael 52
McGarvin, Captain 82
McLean 52
Mier Expedition 47
Mobile, Alabama 68
Morgan, Charles 62
  acquires Texas railroads 95
  becomes largest shareholder in
    Houston Direct Navigation 100
  begins dredging ship channel 100
  death of 103
  establishes bayou port at Clinton 100
  rebuffed by Galveston Wharf
    Company 100
Morgan City, Louisiana 98

INDEX

Morgan Line 86, 98, 100, 109
  complete rail link to Morgan City, Louisiana 107
  places chain across new channel 101

N

Nacogdoches, Texas 11
Neptune 52
Neptune No. 2 65, 67, 72
  collides with *Harriet Lane*, sinks 76
  fitted out as a "cottonclad" 71
  salvaged in place 80
  selected as "cottonclad" 69
New Orleans 43, 60, 79
New York (steamship) 25
nighttime operations on Buffalo Bayou 42
1915 Storm 110
1900 Storm 110
northers 46, 86

O

Ontario 89, 103
Owasco 74, 77
Owl 82

Q

quarantine 87

R

racing 50
  dangers of 50
railroads
  early difficulties of 89
ram fever among Union naval officers 79
Raymond House Hotel, Austin 102
Red Fish Bar 22, 37, 49, 51, 71, 96, 110
Renshaw, William 68
  destroys *Westfield* 79
Rice, William Marsh 49, 86
roads, poor quality of in Texas 12
Rob Roy 86

Ross, John E. 36
Rufus Putnam 39, 41, 102

S

Sam Houston (steamboat) 36, 37
San Antonio, Texas 11, 98
San Felipe, Texas 12
San Jacinto, Battle of 18, 38, 52
San Jacinto Bay 19
San Jacinto River 19
San Jacinto (steamboat) 37
Satilla 112
Schneider, E.B.H. 63, 72
  drills his militia unit 64
  wounded 75
secession 64
Selden, John 37
Sherman, Sidney 52
Sherman, William Tecumseh 85
ship channel
  Federal government buys out Morgan interest in 110
  Federal interest in 109
  first vessel to transit 112
  Houstonians' expectations for 107
Ship Channel Company 99
Shreveport 86
Silver Cloud 83, 86
  at Fort Pillow, Tennessee 86
  service as a Union gunboat 86
  snagged and sunk 86
slaves 45, 56
  labor on steamboats 54
Smith, Frederick 57
Smith, Leon 69, 72, 75
snags 18
South Carolina (U.S. naval vessel) 65
Stanford, Leland 109
St. Clair 84, 86
  service as a Union gunboat 85
Sterrett, Adelle 101
Sterrett, E. Howard 101
Sterrett, Henrietta 61, 101
Sterrett, Ida 101

INDEX

Sterrett, John H. 47, 49, 86
  background of 39
  becomes hotel proprietor in Austin 102
  comes to Texas 41
  death of 102
  experience 59
  Farmer disaster 52
  made C.S. Superintendent of Transports 67
  manner of 102
  purchases new boats 84
  residence in Houston 61
  retires from Houston Direct Navigation 101
  shooting at Warsaw, Kentucky 40
  status report of Texas Marine Department vessels 81
  successfully bids mail contract 57
Sterrett, Josephine 101
Sterrett, Julia 101
Sterrett's Galveston and Houston Daily Line of Steamers 86
Sterrett, Susan Wilson 61, 101
Sterrett, Warner 101
Sterrett, William 101
Sumter, Fort 64
Superior 89, 103
Swenson, Johannes 87

T

Telegraph and Texas Register 34
Texas Marine Department 68, 69
  status of vessels, 1863 81
T.M. Bagby 86, 89, 92
  sold and dismantled 105
Trinity River 52, 93
Turner Rifles 63
Twain, Mark
  on steamboat racing 50

V

Vera Cruz, Mexico 12
Victoria 41

W

Wainwright, Jonathan M. 76
Warsaw, Kentucky 40
Warsaw (steamboat) 36
Webb, Captain 52
Wells, James B. 36
Westfield 77
  blown up 79
Westrop, Thomas 56
Wheeler, John 37
White Oak Bayou 16
Whitney, Charles A. 103
Whitson, Numa M. 56
Wier, Armand 72
  killed 75
Williams, W. Dugat 96
Will o' the Wisp 82

Y

Yellow Stone 34, 36
Young, S.O. 14

ABOUT THE AUTHOR

Andy Hall is a native of Galveston and has spent most of his life on the Texas coast. He spent his early working years, beginning while still an undergrad student, in local history museums, including the Texas Maritime Museum in Rockport. Hall holds degrees from the University of Houston–Clear Lake and Texas Tech University.

For the last twenty years, Hall has served as a volunteer with the Texas Historical Commission in investigating shipwrecks and in 2001 was part of the first group of state marine archaeological stewards appointed in the United States. Hall has worked on numerous marine archaeology projects in Texas, notably from 1995 to 2002 on the *Denbigh* Project, the most extensive excavation and research program on a Civil War blockade runner in the Gulf of Mexico. When he's not working with the Historical Commission on sites in the "Wet Texas" region of the state, he blogs at MaritimeTexas.net, DeadConfederates.com and at the new historical magazine, the *Civil War Monitor*.

www.ingramcontent.com/pod-product-compliance
Lightning Source LLC
Chambersburg PA
CBHW042143160426
43201CB00022B/2388